FINGERPRINTS
and
IMPRESSIONS

FORENSIC EVIDENCE

FINGERPRINTS and IMPRESSIONS

BRIAN INNES

SERIES CONSULTANT: RONALD L. SINGER, M.S.
PRESIDENT, INTERNATIONAL ASSOCIATION OF FORENSIC SCIENCES

Sharpe Focus
an imprint of M.E. Sharpe, Inc.

First edition for the United States, its territories and dependencies,
Canada, Mexico, and Australia, published in 2008 by M.E. Sharpe, Inc.

Sharpe Focus
An imprint of M.E. Sharpe, Inc.
80 Business Park Drive
Armonk, NY 10504

www.mesharpe.com

ISBN: 978-0-7656-8114-0

  Library of Congress Cataloging-in-Publication Data

Innes, Brian.
  Fingerprints and impressions / Brian Innes.
    p. cm. -- (Forensic evidence)
  Includes bibliographical references and index.
  ISBN 978-0-7656-8114-0 (hardcover : alk. paper)
 1. Fingerprints. 2. Fingerprints--Identification. 3. Footprints. 4.
Footprints--Identification. 5. Criminal investigation. 6. Forensic
sciences. I. Title.

HV6074.I56 2008
363.25'8--dc22

                          2007006751

Editorial and design by Amber Books Ltd
Project Editor: Michael Spilling
Copy Editor: Brian Burns
Picture Research: Kate Green
Design: Richard Mason

Cover Design: Jesse Sanchez, M.E. Sharpe, Inc.

Printed in Malaysia

9 8 7 6 5 4 3 2 1

Contents

Introduction

As we approach the end of the first decade of the twenty-first century, interest in the forensic sciences continues to grow. The continued popularity of television shows such as *CSI*, *Crossing Jordan*, *Bones*, and the like has stimulated such an interest in forensic science among middle and high-school students that many schools now offer "forensic science" as a subject choice alongside the more traditional subjects of biology, chemistry, and physics. Each year, the number of colleges and universities offering majors in forensic science at both undergraduate and graduate level has increased, and more and more graduates are entering the job market looking for positions in the forensic science industry. The various disciplines that comprise forensic science provide the opportunity to use education and training in ways that the average student may imagine is rarely possible. On a day-to-day basis, the forensic scientist is called upon to apply the laws of science to the solution of problems that may link a particular individual to a particular crime scene or incident. Alternatively, the same tools and techniques may exonerate an innocent person who has been wrongly accused of committing a crime.

The four books that make up this series—*DNA and Body Evidence*, *Fingerprints and Impressions*, *Fire and Explosives*, and *Hair and Fibers*—are designed to introduce the reader to the various disciplines that comprise the forensic sciences. Each is devoted to a particular specialty, describing in depth the actual day-to-day activities of the expert. The volumes also describe the science behind those activities, and the education and training required to perform those duties successfully. Every aspect of forensic science and forensic investigation is covered, including DNA fingerprinting, crime scene investigation and procedure, detecting trace evidence, fingerprint analysis, shoe and boot prints, fabric prints, ear prints, blood sampling, arson investigation, explosives

Biometric fingerprint scanners are increasingly used for high-security access. Every human fingerprint is unique and virtually impossible to duplicate.

analysis, laboratory testing, and the use of forensic evidence in the courtroom, to cover just a brief sample of what the four volumes of *Forensic Evidence* have to offer. Pull-out feature boxes focus on important aspects of forensic equipment, procedures, key facts, and important case studies.

Numerous criminal cases are described to demonstrate the uses and limits of forensic investigation, including such famous and landmark cases as the O.J. Simpson trial; cases of mistaken identity, such as Will West, who was at first confused with his identical twin and eventually cleared via fingerprint analysis; notorious serial killer Jack Unterweger, who was eventually convicted using DNA analysis from a single hair; and the work of the Innocence Project, which has used DNA analysis to retrospectively overturn wrongful convictions.

In *Fingerprints and Impressions*, the author gives an account of the origins and history of fingerprinting in nineteenth-century police work, fingerprint analysis, glove and fabric prints, impression prints (such as shoes and vehicle tires), and the use of fingerprint evidence in court. Written in a plain, accessible style, the series is aimed squarely at the general reader with an interest in forensic science and crime scene analysis, and does not assume previous knowledge of the subject. All technical language is either explained in the text, or covered in an easy-to-reference glossary on pages 92–93.

Taken as a whole, the *Forensic Evidence* series serves as a comprehensive resource in a highly readable format.

Ronald L. Singer, M.S.
President, International Association of Forensic Sciences

chapter 1

Origins of Fingerprinting

Finger and thumb prints have been used as confirmation of identity since ancient times, but their scientific analysis began only in the late nineteenth century.

It is only very recently that most people have been able to sign their name. In the past, if a signature was needed on a document—perhaps for a will or a lease on a house—a legal official would write in the name, to which the signatory would add an X ("his mark") or a print of the right thumb. This practice dates back many centuries. In ancient China, for example, the "laws of Yung-hwui" (650 C.E.) stated that divorce papers should be signed with prints of the thumb and four fingers. Ancient civilizations in the Middle East and India often used fingerprints to seal official documents.

However, the fingerprint was not intended as a proof of identity. It was merely a confirmation that the person had been present before the legal officer who drew up the document. Even today, someone taking an oath before a notary will be asked to place a finger on the official seal—although not for

◁ **During World War I, the fingerprinting of immigrants and visitors was introduced by the American police after it had shown its worth in criminal investigations.**

9

The skin of the inner hand is covered with tiny ridges in clearly defined patterns. The basis of the fingerprinting technique is that no two individuals have the same pattern.

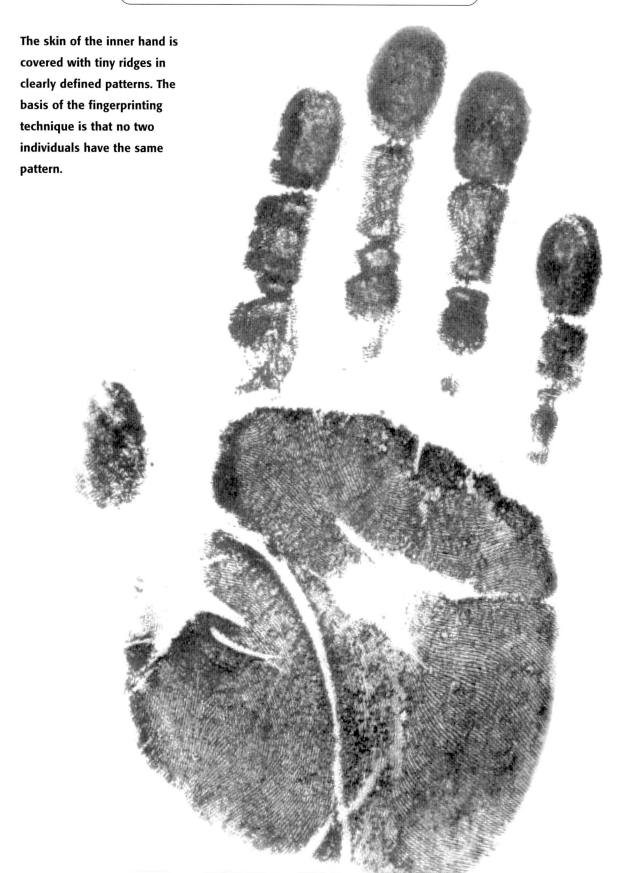

official fingerprinting purposes. And it was not until the late nineteenth century that researchers came to the conclusion that no two people had identical fingerprints, and that this could be a way to establish a person's identity.

The Potter's Thumb

The history of modern fingerprint analysis began with Dr. Henry Faulds. Born in Scotland in 1843, he set up a successful missionary hospital near Tokyo, Japan, in 1874. He was one of the first doctors to introduce Western medicine to Japan. He taught at the local university, where he introduced methods to combat **typhoid** (*tie-foyd*) and lectured on surgery, and he became fluent in Japanese. He was also responsible for founding the Tokyo Institute for the Blind, which exists to this day.

Faulds first became interested in fingerprints when an American **archaeologist**, Edward Morse, began investigating a mound of ancient remains near the hospital. The mound included a large number of pottery fragments. Faulds noticed that the fragments were covered with patterns of lines left by the thumbs and fingers of the potters who had made the pots hundreds of years previously. He then discovered that new pottery on sale in the local market had similar patterns.

The Scottish doctor wondered whether other people had similar fingerprint patterns, so he started to collect the fingerprints of friends, family, students, and local workmen. At first, he made sketches of the patterns, then he used wax to make impressions from people's fingers, and finally he got people to dip their fingers in ink and then press on sheets of paper to leave a pattern. It was then that he discovered that no two patterns were the same.

Faulds soon had thousands of records, but they were all of European or Japanese fingers. He wondered whether people in other countries might also have similar fingerprint characteristics. He wrote to more than a hundred scientists around the world, and sent them a special form that they could use to record all ten **digits**—the eight fingers and both thumbs. Unfortunately, very few wrote back.

Faulds was later able to help solve a crime using his knowledge of fingerprints. Someone attempted to break into the hospital by climbing a whitewashed wall, and left a sooty handprint. The police accused one of his staff, but Faulds convinced them that the handprint on the wall did not match the accused man's handprint. Soon afterward, the true culprit was discovered.

Unique Prints

Faulds quickly realized that the police could use fingerprints to identify criminals and solve crimes. He then decided to prove that every person's prints are unique, and that they do not change with time. He and his students shaved off their fingerprints with razors, and the same pattern grew back each time. The doctor continued his work by studying the fingerprints of Japanese and European children, and showed that they did not change as the children grew. In October 1880, the leading British scientific journal *Nature* published a letter from Faulds that suggested using "bloody finger-marks or impressions on clay [and] glass" to identify criminals. He named his technique **dactylography** (*dak-til-og-ra-fee*) and suggested that a fingerprint record should be kept of all major criminals. But few people showed any interest in his work. Meanwhile, in India, another Briton had also been taking an interest in fingerprints.

Two Rivals

In 1858, William Herschel, just twenty years old, was working as an assistant magistrate for the British government in Bengal, India. He signed a contract allowing a local businessman to supply materials for building roads, and asked the man to seal the contract with an inked print of his hand. Herschel knew that illiterate Indians used smudged fingerprints as signatures. Herschel then began to collect handprints from friends and colleagues. He even asked artists in Calcutta, India, to attempt to make forged copies of handprints—but they failed.

Nearly twenty years later, in 1877, Herschel was made a magistrate in a district outside Calcutta, where his duties included the payment of government pensions. He discovered that relatives of men who had died were still collecting their pensions, so he insisted from then on that each receipt had to be signed with a fingerprint as it could easily be identified. Then, he realized that it would be possible to take fingerprints of prisoners in jail. The fingerprints could be used to identify the prisoners if they escaped and were recaptured, or later arrested for another crime.

KEY FACTS **TELLTALE PATTERN**

The skin on the inner surface of the hands, and on the soles of the feet, is very different from the skin on the rest of the body. It is tougher and covered with tiny ridges—known as **papillary ridges**. In between the ridges, there are tiny **sweat pores**. Although the ridges generally run parallel to one another, they occasionally change direction to form clearly defined patterns.

These papillary ridges begin to form when we are still in the womb, during the third and fourth months of pregnancy. After we are born, the patterns get bigger as our hands and feet grow, but the patterns themselves remain the same. People first knew about papillary ridges as early as the seventeenth century (*see* page 15), but it was another 200 years before anyone realized that each person's pattern of ridges was unique. Even identical twins have prints that are unique only to them as individuals.

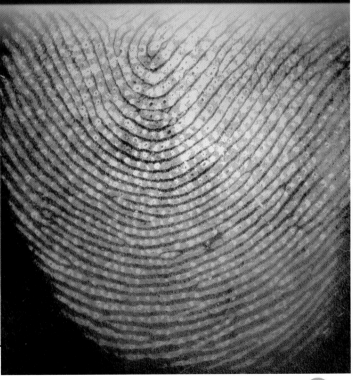

The papillary ridges are very apparent on this computer-generated scan of a thumbprint.

In 1878, Herschel was in bad health, so he returned to England. In 1880, he read Dr. Faulds' letter in *Nature* and wrote a reply, claiming that he was the one who had discovered the technique of fingerprinting. Some time previously, Faulds had also written a letter on the subject to Charles Darwin, the author of *The Origin of Species*.

Darwin passed the letter on to his cousin, Francis Galton, who, unfortunately for Faulds, did nothing with it. Equally unfortunate for Faulds was the fact that Galton was a friend of the Herschel family. One day, Galton and Herschel shared a railway journey together, and Herschel excitedly described his experiences in India. Later, in May 1888, at a lecture Galton gave to the Royal Institution in London, he named Herschel as the man who had discovered fingerprinting. He did mention Faulds's work, but only in passing.

Ever since that time, the popular belief is that Herschel developed the technique of fingerprinting. Few people, apart from forensic historians, remember Faulds and his work. However, by the time he died in 1930, police forces all over the world were using the technique.

Problems of Classification

Herschel did not take his fingerprinting work much further. Galton, however, was now very interested in the subject. In 1884, at the International Health Exhibition in London, he set up his **anthropometric** (*an-throw-po-metric*) laboratory. Here, he examined visitors' height and weight, size of limbs, strength of pull and force of blow, hearing, and ability to distinguish colors. The laboratory's work continued for eight years, with Galton adding people's fingerprints to his growing number of records.

Galton realized that for fingerprinting to be truly useful as a way of identifying individuals, he needed a system of **classification**. He came across a paper published in 1823 by a Czech doctor, Jan Evangelista Purkinje, who had classified fingerprints into nine different types. Though this was significant, Galton knew that it would take a very long time using Purkinje's system to identify individuals by comparing prints.

In 1890, Galton began collecting from people the prints of all ten fingers. He labeled each print with a letter, according to whether the lines rose at one point into an arch (A), formed a loop (L), or gathered into a whorl (W)—where the

KEY FACTS   **FORGOTTEN OBSERVATIONS**

In 1684, Dr. Nehemiah Grew, an English physician, published what is probably the first description of the papillary ridges in the *Philosophical Transactions of the Royal Society*. (The Royal Society was set up in London, England, in 1660, to promote excellence in science. Its work continues to this day.) He noticed what he described as "innumerable little ridges of equal bigness and distance, and everywhere running parallel with one another." As with Dr. Faulds's letter to *Nature* magazine nearly 200 years later, nobody took any interest in what Grew had to say on the subject.

Two years later in Italy, Dr. Marcello Malpighi, a physiologist and professor of anatomy at the University of Bologna, tried to interest his colleagues in the topic. Once again, no one was interested.

A century later, in 1788, J.C.A. Mayers published his illustrated textbook, *Anatomical Copper-Plates with Appropriate Explanations*. He was the first person to point out that the arrangement of skin ridges is never the same on two people. Unfortunately, no one at the time appreciated the significance of this fact.

In 1877, Thomas Taylor, a **microscopist** with the U.S. Department of Agriculture, could have beaten Henry Faulds as the first person to suggest that finger and palm prints could be used for identification in criminal cases. He published reports in two American scientific magazines, but his proposals were not followed up.

Dr. Henry Faulds died in 1930, bitterly disappointed that his pioneering work on fingerprints had been forgotten.

ridges of the fingerprint turn through at least one complete circle. Eventually, Galton recognized that most of the prints in his collection contained a small triangular area where lines ran together—this was particularly true with loops. He named this a "delta"—after Δ, the fourth letter of the Greek alphabet. This meant that if all ten prints were examined, they could quickly be classified—by the four basic types of arch, loop, whorl, and delta—into one out of a possible 1,048,576 combinations. With this many possible variations, there was little chance of the fingerprints of two different people being confused with each other!

Galton, however, used only the two forefingers for analysis, which reduced the number of possible combinations to 60,000. In 1892, he published the results of his researches in his book *Finger Prints*. The title page was decorated with all ten of the author's own fingerprints.

The First Criminal Success

In May 1891, the year before the publication of his book, a scientific journal published a report on Galton's work. Far away in Argentina, Juan Vucetich, Head of the Police Office of Identification and Statistics in La Plata, read the article. It was his job to record the physical details of arrested criminals. After reading the article, he immediately added fingerprints to his records, and began to develop his own system of classification.

The following year, on the evening of June 29, 1892, in Necochea, a tiny village near La Plata, a woman named Francisca Rojas ran screaming from her hut. "My children!" she cried. "He's killed my children!" In the hut, her two children, a boy aged six and a girl aged four, lay dead. Rojas accused a man named Velasquez of the crime. He was jealously in love with her, she claimed. Despite pressure from the local police, Velasquez insisted he was innocent. The police then discovered that Rojas was involved with another man, who had said he would marry her—if she did not have children.

Who was responsible for the horrific murders—Velasquez, the other man, or Rojas herself? The police called in a more experienced officer, Inspector Eduardo Alvarez, who worked under Vucetich in La Plata. Alvarez soon established that Velasquez had an **alibi**, and that the other man had been nowhere near the scene of the crime when it happened.

Sir Francis Galton (1822–1911). A distinguished scientist with many discoveries to his credit, he is now chiefly remembered for his work on fingerprints.

Desperate for clues, Alvarez carefully searched Rojas's hut, and at last spotted a bloody thumbprint on the door. Knowing of Vucetich's work, he cut out a section of the door, took it to the police station, and ordered officers to arrest Rojas. When she arrived at the station, he took prints of both her thumbs and showed her with a magnifying glass how the print of her right thumb matched exactly the thumbprint on the door. Rojas became hysterical, and finally confessed that she had killed her own children to be with the man she loved.

Developing Systems

Between 1891 and 1894, Vucetich worked out the first complete fingerprint classification system. He used the same four basic patterns as Galton, but

The title page of Francis Galton's book _Finger Prints_. Although his analytical method dealt only with two forefingers, all ten of his own prints are featured here.

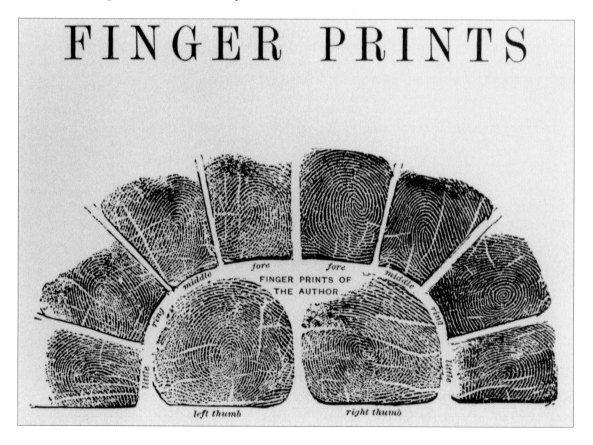

applied them to all ten fingerprints. He also devised ways of subdividing each pattern, and organized his records into small groups that could easily be searched.

By 1894, the Argentine police force had become the first in the world to adopt fingerprinting as the principal means of identifying criminals. Vucetich described his system at the Second Scientific Congress of South America in 1901. Soon, police forces in much of South America had adopted the system. Forces in other parts of the world, however, started to use fingerprinting only a long time after Scotland Yard, England, had adopted the system. Eventually, the English system spread throughout Europe and North America.

The man responsible for the spread was Edward Henry. In 1873, at the age of twenty-three, he was made an assistant magistrate in British India—in the same district, in fact, where Herschel had worked many years previously. Although people largely ignored Herschel's ideas at the time, Henry must have learned something of them. After seventeen years of service, he became inspector general of the Bengal police. He used the standard police method of identifying criminals by their body measurements—anthropometry, or "Bertillonage" (*ber-tee-on-arj*) as it was known, after the Frenchman Louis Adolphe Bertillon, who had developed the system in 1882–1883. In 1893, he read

Sir Edward Henry (1850–1931) developed the system of fingerprint classification that has remained the basis of modern investigation.

Galton's book, *Finger Prints*, and the following year he visited Galton in England and discussed fingerprinting with him. On his return to India, Henry recommended the system to the government of Bengal, pointing out that all it required was a piece of tin and some printer's ink—cheap items, available everywhere. He also added that it would take only a few minutes to learn how to take someone's fingerprints.

Aided by two of his Indian officers, Azizul Haque and Hem Chandra Bose, Henry completed a working system for classifying the prints of all ten digits by 1897. His system was different from Galton's and Vucetich's, however, in that he identified five clearly different types of patterns:

- plain arches (A)
- "tented" arches (T)
- radial loops—inclined toward the outside of the forearm (R)

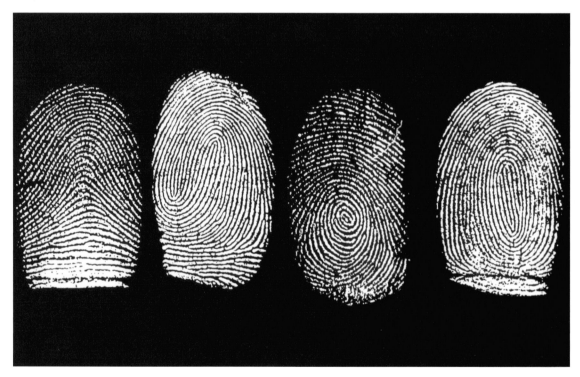

It is remarkable that the significance of different fingerprint patterns was ignored for so long. Featured here are (from left to right) a simple arch, a double loop, a whorl, and a rare pattern of enclosed loop.

- ulnar loops—inclined toward the inner side of the forearm (U)
- whorls (W)

Within a few months, the government of Bengal had adopted Henry's system, and established the first national fingerprint bureau in the world.

CASE STUDY **THE CRIME OF KANGALI CHARAN**

The newly established Bengal fingerprint bureau had its first success very soon. In August 1897, Hriday Nath Ghosh, the manager of a tea garden in northern Bengal, was found in his bedroom with his throat cut. His safe and document box were open and a sum of money was missing. The prime suspect was Kangali Charan, a former cook in the household. He had previously been sentenced to six months in jail for stealing from the same safe—and police had taken his fingerprints.

Among the papers in the document box, Henry's officers found a book with two bloody prints on its cover. The prints matched Charan's. Although he had moved several hundred miles away, he was found and brought to Calcutta, where police took a new print of his right thumb. At his trial for murder and theft, three matching prints were presented to the court.

The judge and two assessors agreed beyond a doubt that the cook had been in Ghosh's bedroom. However, because there were no witnesses to the crime, they decided that the evidence was not strong enough to find Charan guilty of murder. Instead, he was sentenced to two years' hard labor for theft.

The pioneering work of Faulds, Herschel, and Galton, and the careful development of fingerprint classification by Henry, had at last borne fruit. Within only a few years, the technique was to become the most reliable way of identifying an individual, and even today it remains a principal tool of the forensic investigator.

chapter 2

Fingerprinting in England and the United States

After its success in India, the science of fingerprinting was introduced in Britain at London's Scotland Yard. New York soon followed.

In 1893, soon after Sir Francis Galton published his book, *Finger Prints*, an official committee (the Troup Committee) was set up in England to look into ways of identifying people who repeatedly committed crimes. The authorities were already using the anthropometric system (*see* Chapter 1, page 14), but after the committee heard Galton's evidence, they decided to start using fingerprinting as well. Ideally, the committee wanted the police to stop using the anthropometric system altogether and just use fingerprinting. However, at that time, there was still no reliable system of classification. By 1900, it was clear that using both systems was not very effective, so another committee was set up.

The new committee knew about the work Edward Henry had done in India (*see* Chapter 1, page 19), so they called him back to England. Henry had just published his book, *Classification and Uses of Fingerprints*, which impressed the committee.

◁ **By 1950, when this photograph was taken, fingerprinting of suspects had long been standard practice. Here, a U.S. police officer fingerprints a man caught in a raid on a gambling den.**

EMPREINTES DIGITALES
DÉSIGNATIONS ET CLASSIFICATION DES DESSINS

CLASSE e

Sillons en forme de lacets à direction oblique externe (dits en forme d'e) au nombre de 2 au moins.

1 — Forme type e.

2 — Exemple d'e limite avec la classe o (Lacets à direction oblique externe renfermant moins de 4 circuits).

3 — Exemple d'e limite avec la classe u (Empreinte en forme générale d'arcs renfermant 2 lacets à direction oblique externe).

4   5   6 — Autres empreintes ressortissant également à la classe e.

CLASSE i

Sillons en forme de lacets à direction oblique interne (dits en forme d'i) au nombre de 2 au moins.

7 — Forme type i.

8 — Exemple d'i limite avec la classe o (Lacets à direction oblique interne renfermant moins de 4 circuits).

9 — Exemple d'i limite avec la classe u (Empreinte en forme générale d'arcs renfermant 2 lacets à direction oblique interne).

10   11   12 — Autres empreintes ressortissant également à la classe i.

CLASSE o

Sillons en forme d'ovale, de cercle, de spirale ou de volute (dits en forme d'o) comprenant un minimum de 4 lignes circulaires coupées sur la ligne A B (voir fig 29) ou à son défaut A'B' (voir fig 30).

fig 29

fig 30

13 — Type d'o en forme d'ovale.

14 — Type d'o en forme de cercle.

15 — Type d'o en forme de spirale.

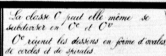
16 — Type d'o en forme de volute double.

La classe o peut elle-même se subdiviser en O^c et O^v.

O^c réunit les dessins en forme d'ovales, de cercles et de spirales.

Sont classées O^v les volutes doubles dans lesquelles on peut retrouver un sillon médian en forme de V qui sépare en deux groupes opposés un ou plusieurs sillons. (Voir n° 21.) Si dans une des boucles du V il n'existait aucun sillon, la volute double restait classée O^c (Voir n° 22).
Exemples :

17 — Exemple d'o limite avec la classe e (Circuits au nombre de 4 au moins entourés de lacets à direction oblique externe).

18 — Exemple d'o limite avec la classe i (Circuits au nombre de 4 au moins entourés de lacets à direction oblique interne).

19   20 — Exemples d'o limites avec la classe u (Empreintes en forme d'arcs dans lesquelles se trouvent au moins 4 circuits centraux).

21 — Volute double comprenant plusieurs sillons entre les boucles du V : à classer O^v.

22 — Volute double ne renfermant aucun sillon entre une des boucles du V : à classer O^c.

CLASSE u

Sillons en forme d'arcs surbaissés (dits en forme d'u) et dessins ne ressortissant à aucune des 3 classes précédentes.

23 — Forme type u.

24 — Exemple d'u limite avec la classe e (Empreinte en forme d'arcs dans laquelle ne se trouve qu'un seul lacet oblique externe).

25 — Exemple d'u limite avec la classe i (Empreinte en forme d'arcs dans laquelle ne se trouve qu'un seul lacet oblique interne).

26 — Exemple d'u limite avec la classe o (Empreinte en forme d'arcs dans laquelle se trouve moins de 4 circuits centraux).

27 — Autre empreinte ressortissant également à la classe u.

28 — Empreinte comprenant à la fois 1 lacet oblique externe, 1 lacet oblique interne, 1 minimum à 3 circuits, et classé u par élimination successive des classes e, i, o.

In 1901, Henry was made Assistant Commissioner of the Metropolitan Police at Scotland Yard in London, and head of the Criminal Investigation Department (CID). Henry immediately began organizing a Fingerprint Department within the CID, and recruited three police officers familiar with the anthropometric system. One of these officers was Detective Sergeant (DS) Charles Collins, who was interested in photography—which was still new at the time. DS Collins realized that it was possible to take photographs of fingerprints at crime scenes. It was not long before he had his first success with this technique.

Evidence in Court

On June 27, 1902, a burglar broke into a house in south London and stole some billiard balls, which were valuable for their ivory. An investigating officer noticed some dirty finger marks on a newly painted windowsill, and contacted the new Fingerprint Department. DS Collins photographed the clearest of the marks— the imprint of a left thumb—and started searching through criminal records. Eventually, he found a match with the prints of Harry Jackson, a forty-one-year-old laborer with a previous conviction for burglary. The police immediately arrested Jackson.

No one had ever presented fingerprint evidence in court before. DS Collins spent a long time explaining the new fingerprinting system to the prosecuting counsel, Richard Muir. When presenting his case in court, Muir carefully explained to the jury how fingerprints had been used successfully to convict criminals in India. DS Collins submitted his photographs, demonstrating how one person's fingerprints could be identified. Faced with this evidence, Jackson's lawyer could not put up much of a defense. The jury found Jackson guilty, and fingerprint evidence was established as part of English law.

Using Henry's classification system, the work of the CID's Fingerprint Department continued to advance. In 1903, Henry, now Police Commissioner, carried out a large-scale experiment. In May, during a major horseracing event, the police arrested sixty men and took their fingerprints. The police quickly discovered that twenty-seven of the men had previous convictions. The men

◁ **This rudimentary chart of fingerprints based on Bertillon's system was used by the French police as early as 1889 to classify fingerprints.**

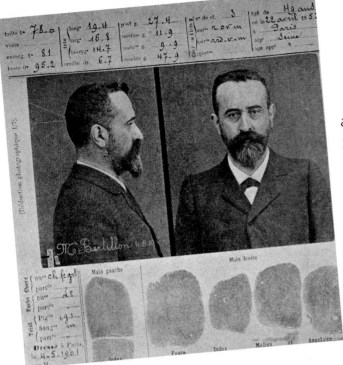

Alphonse Bertillon (1853–1914) developed anthropometry. He also took an interest in fingerprints, but had no method of classifying them.

appeared in court the following morning.

In 1905, fingerprint evidence was used in an English murder case for the first time. On the morning of March 27, Thomas Farrow, the manager of a paint shop in south London, was found battered to death. His wife, who had also been battered, died four days later. Police found an empty cashbox under her bed, with a sweaty print of a right thumb on the inner tray. The police suspected two local small-time criminals, Alfred and Albert Stratton. The print turned out to be Alfred's. Once again, Richard Muir was the prosecuting lawyer, and Collins—now Detective Inspector—presented his detailed photographs and fingerprint records to the court.

In a clear sign that fingerprint evidence was still in its early days, the judge suggested to the jury that this evidence alone might not be enough for a clear verdict. Despite this, the jury found both Stratton brothers guilty, and recommended the death sentence.

Fingerprinting in the United States

In the United States, up to the end of the nineteenth century, there was little interest in using fingerprints to identify criminals—because there was no practical system of classification. Then, about 1881, a detective from California, Harry Morse, advised the authorities to register immigrant Chinese laborers by taking their thumbprints. Although this did not happen, the superintendent of the San Francisco Mint, Franklin Lawton, liked the idea and asked the landscape photographer Isaiah W. Taber to start photographing laborers' thumbs. However, by 1888, Congress had banned any more Chinese workers from entering the United States, so there was no longer any need for registration.

Then, in 1904, at the St. Louis World's Fair, Britain erected a Royal Pavilion on the fairgrounds to display some of the gifts Queen Victoria had received for her Diamond Jubilee (Victoria had been Queen for sixty years). One of the British police officers guarding the display was DS John Ferrier of Scotland Yard's

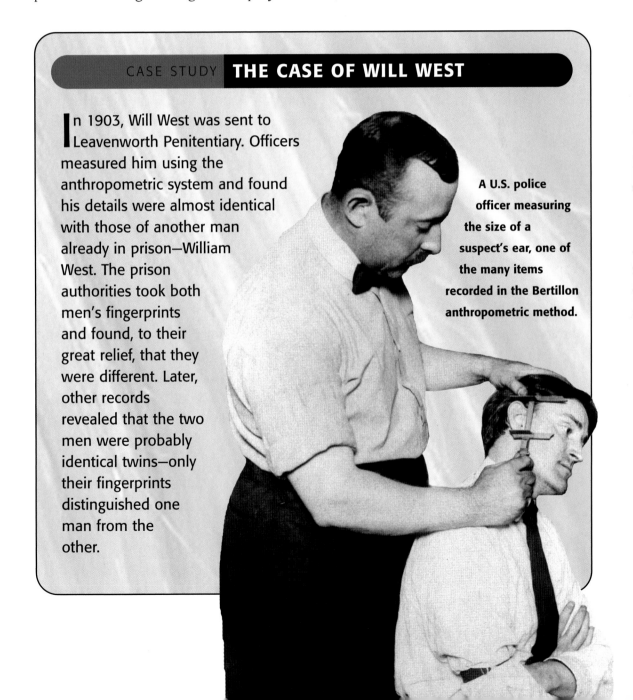

CASE STUDY **THE CASE OF WILL WEST**

In 1903, Will West was sent to Leavenworth Penitentiary. Officers measured him using the anthropometric system and found his details were almost identical with those of another man already in prison—William West. The prison authorities took both men's fingerprints and found, to their great relief, that they were different. Later, other records revealed that the two men were probably identical twins—only their fingerprints distinguished one man from the other.

A U.S. police officer measuring the size of a suspect's ear, one of the many items recorded in the Bertillon anthropometric method.

Fingerprint Department. In his time in the United States, he gave several demonstrations of the Henry fingerprinting classification system, and managed to convince one important police official in New York of its value in solving crimes. He, in turn, convinced others and, before long, New York had its own fingerprint department.

About the same time, the U.S. Department of Justice started looking at the possibility of using fingerprints to identify criminals. The Department gave a small amount of money to set up a system at Leavenworth Penitentiary in Kansas. In 1905, Sing Sing and other prisons in New York State started to use the technique, and the St. Louis police adopted it the following year.

Following the success of the Henry classification system, the Army, Navy, and Marine Corps began fingerprinting servicemen. As the number of records held by separate organizations grew rapidly, it became clear that it would be better to keep all records in one place for classification and analysis. The Department of Justice instructed Leavenworth Penitentiary to carry out the work.

Accepted in Law

Fingerprint evidence had not yet been accepted in U.S. law—though that was about to change. Shortly after 2 A.M. on the morning of September 19, 1910, Clarence Hillier encountered an intruder on the stairs of his Chicago home. He fought with the man, and in the struggle both fell down the stairs. Hillier's wife heard two shots, and the front door slam as the intruder fled. In the hallway, she found her husband dead.

Soon after, four off-duty police officers on their way home saw a man behaving suspiciously less than a mile from the Hillier home. They stopped and searched him, finding a loaded revolver in his trouser pocket. The man's left arm was bleeding—he claimed he had fallen off a streetcar. He told the officers he was Thomas Jennings, and willingly went with them to the station. At the station, the officers heard about the murder of Clarence Hillier. They then discovered that Jennings was on parole from Joliet Penitentiary, where he had been serving a sentence for burglary.

Investigators searched the Hillier home and found an impression of four left-hand fingers on the newly painted railing of the back porch. They matched, in every detail, the prints taken from Jennings on his arrest, and those in his prison

J. Edgar Hoover takes the prints of Vice President John Nance Garner in 1939. President Franklin Roosevelt had suggested that all members of Congress, and White House employees, should be fingerprinted.

record. At his trial, four experts testified that the fingerprint identification could not be disputed. Jennings was found guilty and sentenced to death. His lawyers appealed to the Illinois Supreme Court, claiming that the fingerprint evidence could not be accepted under state law, and that the experts were not qualified. However, on December 21, 1911, the Supreme Court decided that the fingerprint evidence was legal, and confirmed Jennings's sentence.

Fingerprinting and the FBI

Since 1896, the International Association of Chiefs of Police, which was made up of the heads of police departments in most large U.S. cities and Canada, had established a National Bureau of Criminal Identification. The Bureau was located first in Chicago, and later moved to Washington, D.C. Later, when the Bureau had gathered a vast number of fingerprint records, it persuaded the Department of Justice to set up a central government fingerprint bureau.

The obvious choice was the Federal Bureau of Investigation (FBI), which had just been created. In 1921, a criminal identification department was set up within the FBI. For several years it achieved little because it did not have enough money. Then, in May 1924, J. Edgar Hoover became head of the FBI. Two months after he took up his post, Congress gave Hoover $56,000 to equip and operate the department. Hoover immediately set about getting the records in order—by that time, there were more than 800,000 piled up in various storage areas. It took eight years to organize them.

From the beginning, Hoover also believed it was important to include in the FBI's files the fingerprints of people who had no criminal connections. He argued that they could be used to trace missing persons, identify the mutilated victims of disasters, confirm the identity of people involved in civil disputes, and prove people's innocence. The U.S. Civil Service Commission turned over to the FBI its files of employees and people who had applied for employment, adding thousands of new fingerprints to the FBI's files. In 1931, Hoover informed the House Appropriations Committee (which is responsible for setting federal budgets) that he had the largest identification bureau in the world. In his time as head of the FBI, Hoover used his files to harass and threaten innocent people and his political enemies. Despite this abuse of power, no one doubts the importance of the FBI's vast files in solving crime.

KEY FACTS · IDENTIFYING MISSING PERSONS

The FBI's files are full of unusual cases. In one case, fingerprint experts had to identify a hand found in the stomach of a shark caught off the coast of Florida. It turned out that the hand belonged to a sailor who had drowned when a U.S. Navy vessel sank.

The FBI has also solved many cases involving people with amnesia (loss of memory). For example, a woman walked into a police station in Indiana not knowing who she was or where she lived. Police soon identified her from prints taken years before when she had applied for government work, and reunited her with her family. In another case, a young man who could not remember who he was, turned out to have enlisted in the Navy eleven years earlier. Finally, a California policeman, who had disappeared while on duty, was eventually found in Montana after the authorities circulated his prints.

Before the introduction of computerization, fingerprint records had to be examined, one by one, by hand—a long and exhausting procedure.

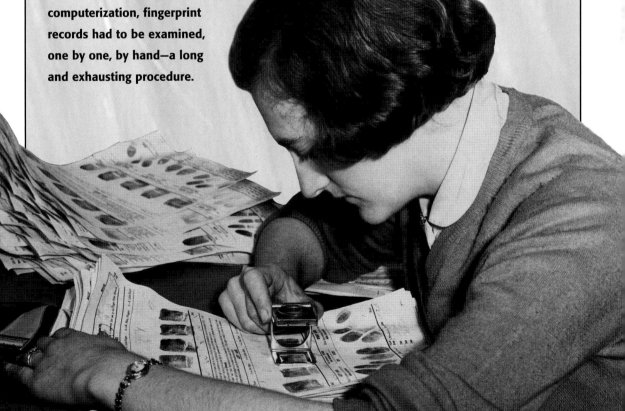

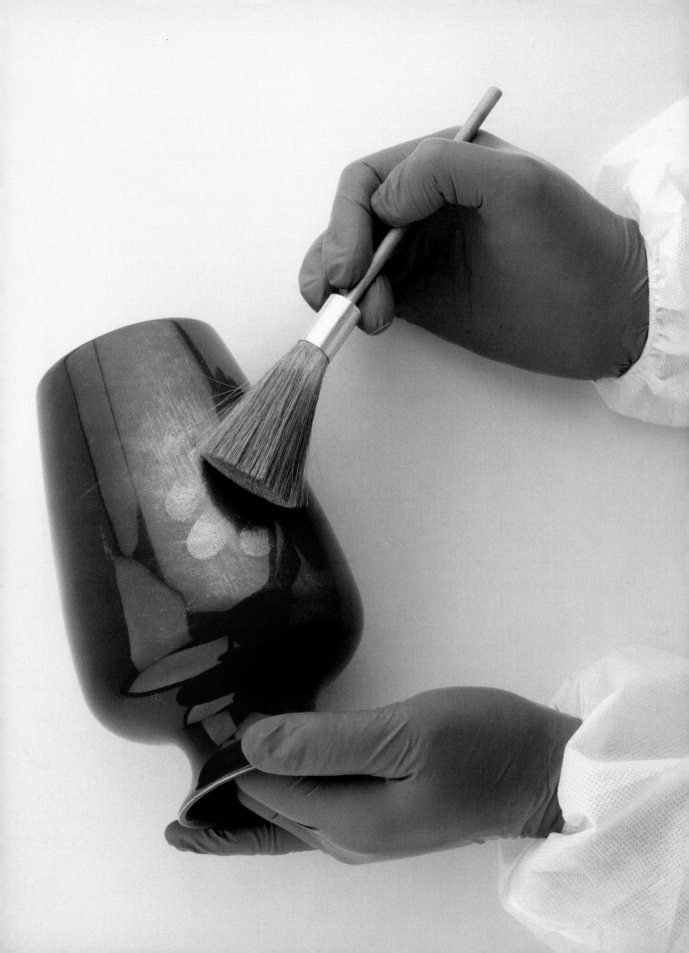

chapter 3

Examining the Evidence

The detection and analysis of fingerprints is a time-consuming operation, but it provides vital evidence in solving many crimes.

Fingerprints are divided into two types. The first are visible prints, also known as **patent prints**, which are made when someone transfers blood, soot, ink, paint, or similar fluid material from their fingers onto a plain surface, or when they press their fingers into a soft material such as clay or fresh paint. Visible prints were the first kind that investigators were able to examine. They soon discovered, however, that there were other prints which were not immediately visible—**latent prints**. Investigators use special methods to detect latent prints.

Latent prints are left as minute traces of sweat, either directly from the fingertips themselves, or after the fingers have accidentally touched the face or another sweaty part of the body. They weigh between 4 and 250 micrograms, and are 99 percent water. The remaining 1 percent is a complex mixture of substances, which varies from person to person, and from

◁ **Revealing prints on a ceramic vase by dusting with a camel-hair brush. The investigator wears full scene-of-crime clothing to avoid the risk of contaminating the evidence.**

33

A police officer lifting fingerprints with adhesive tape after a 2003 bank robbery in Syracuse, New York. They may have been left not by the robbers but by an innocent person, who must be eliminated from the investigation.

hour to hour in the same person. Fingerprint investigators, however, are more interested in the fact that a latent print can be almost permanent. Investigators have even managed to lift latent prints from objects in ancient tombs.

At a crime scene, it is vital to search for latent prints. Investigators must take the fingerprints of any victims—surviving or dead—in order to eliminate them from the investigation. At any crime scene, investigators will almost certainly find "unknown" prints. They may be from innocent people who were at the scene before the crime was committed, or who arrived at the scene and contacted the police. It is also possible for the first officers at the scene, or the paramedic crew (if they are called to remove an injured or dead person), to leave their prints accidentally. When investigators have taken fingerprints from all these people, the remaining "unknown" prints may lead them to the criminal.

Latent prints can be "developed" in a variety of ways. The original technique, still in use today, is to dust the prints with a very fine powder, using a camel-hair brush or an "insufflator"—a device like an old-fashioned scent spray, with a flexible bulb to blow the powder through a narrow nozzle.

CASE STUDY **A FORMER NAZI DETECTED**

In 1975, the U.S. Department of Justice wanted to deport Valerian Trifa, a former archbishop of the Romanian Orthodox Church. Department officials believed that when he entered the United States, Trifa hid the fact that, before 1945, he had been a member of the Iron Guard, Romania's pro-Nazi party. He denied the charge, but in 1982 the then West German government found in its archives a postcard that Trifa had written forty years earlier to a high-ranking Nazi official.

The Germans would not allow the FBI to use chemicals or powders on this important historic document, but laser illumination revealed Trifa's thumbprint, and he was deported in 1984.

Former Romanian archbishop Valerian Trifa, deported by the U.S. Department of Justice in 1984.

In the early days of fingerprinting, the powder was a mixture of liquid mercury and chalk ground finely together. However, mercury vapor is very poisonous, so investigators now use other materials. Prints on glass, silver, and dark shiny surfaces are revealed with a light gray powder. Prints on light-colored, smooth surfaces are dusted with black powder. Colored and fluorescent powders can also be used.

A newer device, the MagnaBrush, uses magnetic powders. Small particles attach themselves to the print, and the rest is removed using a magnet. Magnetic brushes are used only on **nonferrous** (containing no iron) surfaces. However, the inventor of the brush, forensic scientist Dr. Herbert MacDonnell, claims that it can also be effective on **ferrous** (containing iron) materials.

Prints on porous (full of tiny holes) materials, such as many types of paper, cardboard, or wood, must be developed in a different way. For many years, investigators used a solution of **silver nitrate** or **iodine vapor**. The silver nitrate reacts with the salt in the sweat, and the iodine vapor reacts with the grease. However, in 1954, forensic scientists discovered that traces of **amino acids** in sweat react with a chemical called **ninhydrin** (*nin-hahy-drin*), and developed a new method. First, investigators spray the material containing the print with a solution of ninhydrin. Then, they dry it in an oven, revealing purplish latent prints. Other similar methods use dyes that react with the

Before being lifted and sent for comparison with existing records, fingerprints must be examined to ensure they are not smudged.

proteins in sweat. It can take a long time to find latent prints, because the entire crime scene must be examined. An accidental—but very important—discovery was that prints exposed to the fumes of "superglue" (**cyanoacrylate**) show up white on darker surfaces. This method is extremely useful when examining enclosed spaces, such as cupboards and the interiors of cars. Any prints discovered can then be dusted or photographed. Researchers in a Canadian laboratory made another accidental discovery: laser beams reveal latent prints. Unlike dusting powders or chemicals, lasers do not affect the material containing the prints, and seem to be most effective on older evidence.

Other Modern Developments

It is also possible to develop latent prints from items using a method known as "vacuum deposition of metal vapors." The metals used can be lead, gold, or silver used in combination with cadmium or zinc. The primary metals react with the cadmium or zinc to reveal the print. The item with the print is placed in a chamber facing a dish containing the combined metals, and then all the air is pumped out of the chamber. The metals are heated to a high temperature until they vaporize—that is, begin to soften and turn to liquid. A thin layer then settles on the surface of the item. This technique is particularly useful when developing latent prints from materials such as plastics—it is very difficult to get prints from plastics using chemicals or powders.

Another method uses **radioactive** gas, and does not destroy the evidence. The article is placed in an airtight chamber filled with a small amount of the gas, which reacts with the print. Although the result is not visible, the print is now radioactive. Investigators then use X-ray sensitive film, which they develop in the normal way to reveal the prints.

Even when it is possible to preserve a piece of material containing fingerprint evidence, the prints themselves are photographed. For many years, latent prints were also photographed. Today, they are usually "lifted" (taken from the surface) with transparent adhesive tape, which is then mounted on a transparent backing, or on a piece of colored card. Investigators also use a very shiny paper called Kromecote (*kroh-ma-koht*) and special X-ray techniques to lift prints from skin. These prints can be valuable evidence, particularly in cases of physical attack, but they do not usually survive for more than an hour or two.

Single Print System

The fingerprint examiner's first job is to eliminate all the innocent people who have been at the crime scene. Although investigators increasingly use computer technology, they also still use conventional methods. Two sets of prints are taken on a standard form, which has labeled spaces for each finger. First, they ink all ten digits one by one and roll each one from edge to edge in the appropriate space, to ensure that they record the patterns extending around the curve of the finger. Then, the same ten prints are taken as "plain" impressions, without rolling. Fingerprinting a dead body is usually a routine process, similar to taking prints from a living person.

Sometimes, however, investigators have to be a bit more inventive. In 1938, the decomposing body of a woman was found in the sea off the coast of

◁ **Chief Superintendent Frederick Cherrill, who headed Scotland Yard's fingerprint department from 1938 to 1953.**

▷ **The intense manual examination of fingerprint records, before computerization, is typified in this crowd of FBI specialists at work in the Bureau's Fingerprint Identification Division.**

Cornwall, western England. Her fingertips had been worn smooth by sand and gravel. Chief Superintendent (CS) Frederick Cherrill, who was then the leading fingerprint expert at Scotland Yard, peeled the skin from her hands—as if he were pulling off a pair of tight gloves. On the underside, her prints were intact—though in reverse.

From the beginning of police fingerprinting, comparing, and identifying prints was a slow, difficult task. With thousands of record cards to check, police authorities realized that they needed a new classification system. This was particularly essential when only a single print was available.

In 1927, at Scotland Yard, Detective Chief Inspector (DCI) Harry Battley introduced a new filing system. He took a fixed-focus magnifying glass and had a glass base engraved with seven concentric circles (circles with a common center), with **radii** from 0.12 inches (3 mm) to 0.6 inches (15 mm), identified by the letters A to G.

By positioning the glass over what appeared to be the center of the fingerprint pattern (the "core"), it was easy to classify any delta (*see* Chapter 1, page 16) by the circle in which it could be found. A separate collection of prints was made for each digit. Each of the ten collections was then divided into nine sub-classifications:

- arch
- tented arch
- radial loop
- ulnar loop
- whorl (the original Henry types)
- double loop
- pocket loop (with a tiny whorl at its center)
- composite
- accidental (similar to a double loop, but with one loop enclosing a tiny pocket)

Then, each print was further classified by its delta. Other police forces soon adopted this Single Print System and it remains the basis of all fingerprint classification today. Despite the greatly improved Single Print System, it was still an enormous task to sort through millions of records. In the twentieth century,

Some examples of the more detailed classification of different types of fingerprint, illustrated in the Federal Bureau of Investigation's handbook, *The Science of Fingerprints*.

Plain arch

Tented arch

Loop

Double loop

Double loop with delta

Plain whorl

"Accidental"

Central pocket loop

many police forces stopped dusting for prints in cases such as thefts from cars or homes. And when they did dust, it was only to reassure the public that they were being thorough. The truth was that if the prints obtained from a crime scene were not already on file, the search for a match could be pointless.

On the other hand, it was easy for police to match prints as soon as they had detained a suspect, since his or her prints could be matched with existing records. For this reason, police investigating major crimes, such as rape, murder, and abduction, take the fingerprints of entire local populations when they suspect that the perpetrator is among them. This may still involve the checking of thousands of prints, but they are still only a small proportion of the millions on record.

The Digital Age

It is much easier to search through fingerprint records by using computer databases. If an unknown print has been lifted from a crime scene, it takes computers only a few minutes to find a match—as long, of course, as it is in the database. Some computer systems can make up to 30,000 comparisons per second.

About twenty years ago, the Federal Bureau of Investigation (FBI) set up an entirely electronic program—the Automated Fingerprint Identification System (AFIS). Thanks to AFIS, there is almost no need now for fingerprint cards. Local police forces scan fingers and transmit the digital images to the state identification bureau. If the local bureau cannot find a match, it transmits the images to the FBI's Identification Division. As soon as the Identification Division comes up with any information, it contacts the local police within minutes.

Currently, the FBI holds approximately 250 million fingerprint records. More than 100 million of them are in criminal files, and the rest are mainly from FBI checks on applicants for federal employment. In Canada, the Royal Canadian Mounted Police database has approximately 4 million prints on record, and other countries are rapidly catching up. Very soon, it will be possible, using digitized images, to match prints from anywhere in the world.

With modern computer technology, it is also possible to enhance faint or slightly smudged prints, making them easier to analyze.

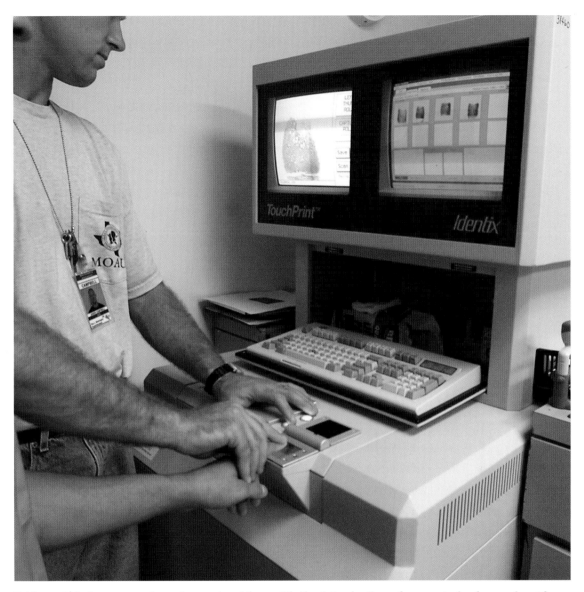

Taking prints is now much easier, and quicker, with the introduction of computerized scanning. The recorded prints can then be transmitted to the FBI for comparison with records.

Some Surprising Successes

The FBI was sent the clothing of a woman who had been tortured and killed. One examiner noticed an unusual pattern in the fabric of her pantyhose, and when he looked closely, he realized that a fingerprint had been burned into the material. He learned that the woman had been tortured with a hot knife and that the killer had wrapped the pantyhose around the knife to avoid burning his hand. The fabric had melted in the heat, and the killer left his fingerprint on it. This evidence contributed to his conviction.

In England, a woman was attacked in the street, but successfully defended herself. In the hospital, the doctor examining her noticed a fragment of skin between two of her teeth. The woman remembered biting at her attacker's fingers, and the doctor notified the police.

Some hours later, a man with a bandaged left middle finger was brought in for questioning. A piece of skin had been torn from the tip. Although he claimed he had injured it at work, a fingerprint expert proved that the fragment taken from the woman's teeth fitted exactly into the tear mark.

Solving the Pieces of the Puzzle

In 1990, police in Miami, Florida, arrested a suspect in a drug case. His fingertips were badly scarred because he had sliced the skin from them, cut it into small pieces, and transplanted the pieces onto other fingertips, turning himself into a "forensic jigsaw puzzle." An FBI expert spent weeks solving the problem. He made enlarged photographs of the man's jumbled prints, cut them in pieces, and eventually matched up the ridge patterns to produce a set of the original prints. They corresponded with a wanted man's prints.

In 1941, an American criminal named Roscoe James Pitts had the skin removed from his fingertips, and then sewn to his chest until they healed, without any ridge pattern reappearing on his fingers. However, his original print record, and the prints taken when he was later arrested, included portions of the ridge pattern below the first finger joint. This was enough to make a positive identification.

In November 1943, two workers discovered the body of a woman in a river near Luton in southern England. There was no means of identifying the woman, and her fingerprints matched nothing in police files. She had been badly beaten about the head, and in the post-mortem photographs, her face was unrecognizable. Three months later, a piece of a black coat, with a dyer's label attached, was discovered on a garbage dump. The dyeing company confirmed that it had taken an order eleven months earlier from a woman named Irene

CASE STUDY **THE NIGHT STALKER**

Between June 1984 and August 1985, a serial killer dubbed by local newspapers as the "Night Stalker" haunted the suburbs of Los Angeles. Usually, he would break into homes after midnight, then assault and kill his victims. Most of the Night Stalker's victims were killed with a shot to the head. A few, however, survived, and were able to describe their attacker to the police. One of the victims even saw her attacker drive away in a battered orange Toyota, which was later found abandoned. Laser scanning revealed a single latent fingerprint on the rear-view mirror.

Just a few days before, the state criminal computer in Sacramento had been updated with all the fingerprints on file of people born since January 1, 1960. Thanks to this stroke of good luck, police identified the fingerprint from the mirror. It belonged to Richard Ramirez, a drifter, age twenty-five, with two convictions for car theft. Ramirez was born on February 28, 1960.

Photographs of the wanted man were published throughout the state. Ramirez, who had been in El Paso, Texas, returned to Los Angeles to find his likeness on the front pages of all the newspapers in the first store he entered. Local people recognized him and chased him until he gave himself up to a passing patrol car.

Richard Ramirez, the Night Stalker. At his trial he boasted: "I am beyond good or evil.... Lucifer dwells in us all."

Manton. No one had seen Irene since the previous November. Her husband Bertie claimed that she had left home after a quarrel and was now living in London.

For some time, many police forces gave up dusting for prints in minor cases of vehicle theft, because identification was too time-consuming. However, the introduction of computerization has resulted in the technique being reintroduced.

Chief Superintendent (CS) Cherrill searched the Manton home, hoping to find a fingerprint to match the victim's, but everything had been thoroughly cleaned—even the empty glass jars and bottles in the cellar. Then, in a corner, he found one bottle covered with dust. In the dust was a print matching the left thumbprint of the dead woman. Bertie Manton confessed to his wife's murder and was sentenced to life imprisonment.

The Triple Fingerprint Triumph

On February 9, 1996, a huge bomb exploded in the center of London's Docklands, killing two newspaper sellers, injuring about forty people, and causing a lot of damage—all that was left was a large crater. A police officer, however, had noticed a truck parked on the spot where the explosion occurred. It was a Ford flatbed, adapted to transport cars. When a drawing of the car was published, someone telephoned the police to say that he had seen such a vehicle parked on an industrial park a few days earlier.

Police searched the site and found a pile of garbage containing a set of Northern Ireland license plates, tachograph charts (which record the details of the journeys a vehicle makes), magazines, and a meal voucher from a Northern Ireland ferry.

The tachograph charts provided details of the truck's movements during the previous four months. It had been bought in Carlisle, northwest England, taken to Northern Ireland, and then brought back to England. It turned out that the driver and his friend had stayed twice at the same Carlisle motel. Although the room had been cleaned many times, fingerprint officers were able to lift about 100 prints. After eliminating the staff's prints, they were left with a single unknown thumbprint on an ashtray.

At the same time, experts at Scotland Yard found thumbprints on one of the magazines that matched the print on the ashtray. However, they could find no match in criminal records, and the investigation came to a temporary standstill. Finally, in April 1997, an Irish Republican Army unit was captured in Northern Ireland. One of the unit members was James McArdle, a truck driver. His thumbprint matched that of the bomber the police had by now dubbed the "Triple Fingerprint Man." In 1998, he was sentenced to twenty-five years in prison.

CASE STUDY · THE MURDER OF JUNE DEVANEY

The most outstanding example of mass fingerprinting—and probably unique in its extent and the dedication of the police officers who undertook it—happened in the town of Blackburn, northern England.

At midnight on May 14, 1948, three-year-old June Devaney was asleep in the children's ward of a hospital in Blackburn. Just over an hour later, the nurse on night duty discovered that the little girl was no longer in her cot. On the floor beside it was a large glass bottle. Despite a frantic search of the hospital and its immediate surroundings, there was no sign of her. Hospital staff called the police, who found the girl's tiny body close to the boundary wall of the hospital grounds. She had been brutally attacked and battered to death against the wall.

The police lifted ten prints from the bottle, which did not match any of the hospital staff. They were from the thumb, four fingers, and palm of a left hand, and two fingers of the right hand, together with three partial prints. The prints were broad, clear, and detailed, and showed no scars or signs of coarsening. The police concluded that they belonged to a well-built young man who had done little or no heavy manual work.

Investigators took the fingerprints of every male over sixteen who had been in Blackburn on the night of May 14–15. In total, they collected almost 50,000 prints. After two months of house-to-house inquiries, they temporarily halted the operation to allow officers to check through more than 40,000 records—with no luck, unfortunately. On August 9, they resumed their inquiry and three days later one of the officers found a match.

The prints belonged to Peter Griffiths (pictured, right), a former soldier, aged twenty-two. He was record number 46,253. He confessed to his horrific crime and was hanged in November of the same year.

A fireman examines the damage to nearby businesses following the Docklands bombing in London in 1996. Successful identification of fingerprints proved essential in bringing the criminals to justice.

Palm Prints

After Detective Chief Inspector (DCI) Battley had introduced his Single Print System in 1927, he and Chief Superintendent (CS) Cherrill turned their attention to palm prints. The ridge patterns of the rest of the hand are as distinctive as fingerprints. At first, palm prints were filed together with their related fingerprints, and it was some time before anyone introduced a separate plan of classification.

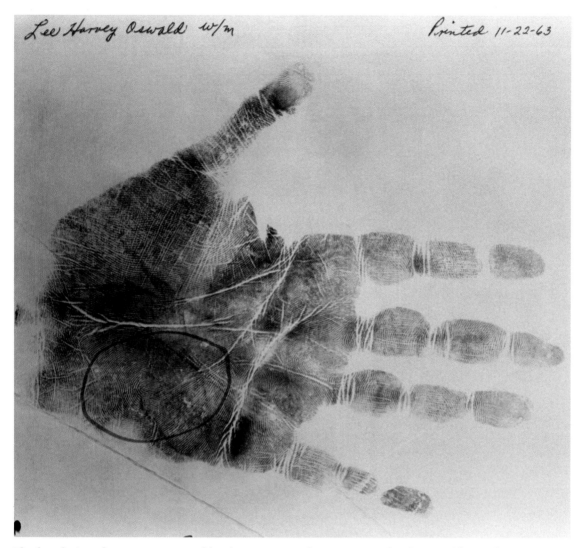

Lee Harvey Oswald w/m   *Printed 11-22-63*

The handprint of Lee Harvey Oswald, taken on November 23, 1963, the day President John F. Kennedy was assassinated. The circle surrounds a print fragment found on a box at the site where the bullets were fired.

However, CS Cherrill soon demonstrated the importance of palm prints. In 1931, a burglar named John Egan broke into a number of houses in the London suburbs. During one break-in, he left his handprint on a glass tabletop. There were only fragments of his fingerprints, but these were enough to identify him as a suspect. He was arrested, and CS Cherrill took his palm print. Faced with this strong evidence, Egan pleaded guilty, so CS Cherrill was not called to testify in court. It was not until 1942 that CS Cherill was able to have palm print evidence established in English law.

In the same year, intruders beat an elderly pawnbroker to death with a revolver butt at his London premises, and rifled the safe. CS Cherrill found a single palm print on the safe door, but could not trace it in the records. However, the police investigation led to the arrest of one George Silverosa, whose palm print was a perfect match.

Silverosa admitted his part in the crime, but claimed an accomplice, Sam Dashwood, was the murderer. The two prints were submitted in evidence and, when both men refused to speak in their defense, they were found guilty and sentenced to death. Many similar cases soon followed, and many police forces around the world now keep palm print records.

CASE STUDY **MURDER ON THE GOLF COURSE**

In April 1955, Mrs. Elizabeth Currell did not return home from walking her dog on a local golf course on the outskirts of London, England. Her body was found at dawn the next day. She had been battered to death with a heavy iron tee-marker, on which the police found a partial palm print in blood. At that time, Scotland Yard had approximately 6,000 palm prints on file, but none provided a match with the print on the tee-marker.

The police carried out a mass hand-printing operation among all the males who lived or worked close by. The teams examining the prints were allowed to work alternate weeks, in order to avoid straining their eyes too much. After two months, they had gathered almost 9,000 prints. Then, after a long, painstaking search, officers positively identified record number 4605. They had taken it a few weeks previously from Michael Queripel, age eighteen.

At first, Queripel claimed that he had come across Mrs. Currell's body by accident, but he later confessed to her murder. At that time, England had not yet abolished the death penalty for murder, but Queripel avoided it by just a few days. At the time of the murder he had been only seventeen, so he was sentenced to long-term imprisonment.

chapter 4

Glove and Fabric Prints

Even when a criminal has taken care to leave no fingerprints at a crime scene, there are other evidence traces that can lead to his or her identification.

A s soon as criminals learned that the police could use fingerprints to identify the perpetrators of crime, many started wearing gloves to avoid detection. Sometimes, however, they were careless, still leaving behind the vital evidence that pointed to them.

In Manchester, England, during the 1970s, a man wearing surgical gloves broke into a post office, confident that he would leave no identifiable traces. However, as he was leaving the premises, he took off the gloves and threw them on the floor. By turning the gloves inside out, the police fingerprint expert obtained a complete set of clear prints from the inner surface. On another occasion, a burglar took a new pair of rubber gloves to the crime scene. They were held together by a paper band, which he stripped off—leaving a perfect set of his prints on the surface.

◁ **Fingerprints revealed on the inner surface of a rubber glove by the use of a magnetic brush.**

In 1962, there was a similar case involving a break-in at a London art gallery. Two thieves carried off works by Degas, Renoir, Matisse, and Picasso. They also wore new rubber gloves but, without thinking, they threw the packaging into the garbage, leaving prints for the police.

Even perpetrators who wear gloves while committing a crime often forget that the car they drive away in, or the base they operate from, are probably covered in prints. When a gang stole £2,500,000 (equivalent to $3,500,000 U.S.) in Britain's 1963 Great Train Robbery, they left their fingerprints all over the remote farm building that they had used as a hideout—enough evidence for nine convictions.

An expert witness in the O. J. Simpson murder trial demonstrates that the bloodstained gloves presented in evidence could not match the size of Simpson's hands.

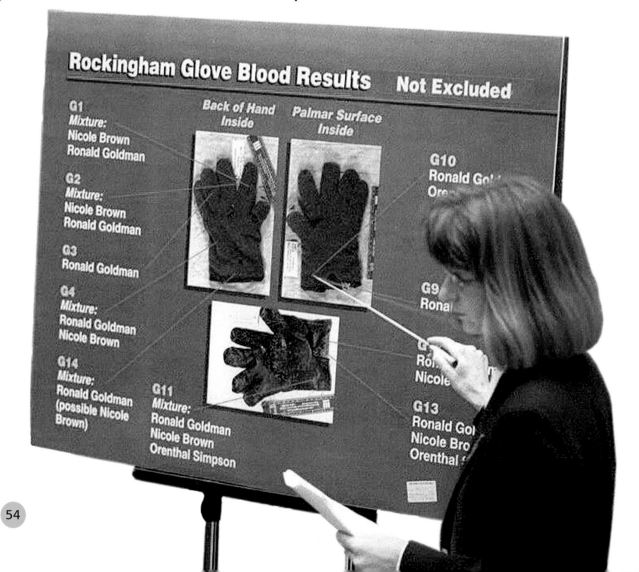

Glove Prints

However, even the police would admit that these were lucky breaks. Gerald Lambourne, head of Scotland Yard's Fingerprint Department, 1975–1980, wondered whether it was possible to identify prints left by gloves. In 1956, he began to research the subject. In his book *The Fingerprint Story* (1984), he wrote that gloves pick up dirt and grease from everyday items such as doorknobs, rails, doors, and train seats. Gradually, this dirt and grease builds into a dense layer, which leaves its own print on objects. Although not as strong or clear as fingerprints, glove prints can sometimes be relied on to identify and trace criminals.

A special solution has been used to enhance ridge detail in a palm print found in blood on a bed sheet. This process emphasizes ridge detail but stains the fabric blue.

Over the years, Lambourne consulted the National Association of Glove Manufacturers, the British Plastic Federation, and the Leather Institute. He watched gloves being cut, sewn, and molded, and studied the wide variety of materials used in their manufacture. He was particularly interested in ordinary household latex rubber gloves. Theoretically, these gloves—thousands of them—all have a standard grip pattern on their tips. With the manufacturers'

PROCEDURE COMPARING PRINTS

Unlike fingerprints, glove prints cannot be collected on a database. Because the print left by an individual glove will be different from that of any other, it is necessary to have a glove obtained from a suspect for comparison. In his book *Techniques of Crime Scene Investigation* (1992), Barry A. J. Fisher, who was director of the Scientific Services Bureau, Los Angeles County Sheriff's Department, described how the comparison should be carried out.

Investigators have to compare glove prints found at crime scenes with a suspect's gloves. The investigator puts on each glove and leaves a print on glass—the ideal surface for showing up prints. Sometimes, however, it is necessary to use the same material as the material containing the print found at the crime scene.

Investigators must also decide how the suspect's hand touched or gripped the evidence material. They then make the comparison print in the same way, and they may need to experiment a few times. To make an accurate comparison, they also have to estimate how much pressure was involved in making the print at the crime scene, and then use the same amount of pressure to make the comparison print.

Glove prints are generally fainter than fingerprints, so investigators must develop them with great care. First, they search the prints with a laser, or a similar specialized, high-powered light source, and then dust them lightly. It is not possible to lift the developed print, so it must be photographed as soon as possible. Investigators have successfully treated rubber gloves with ninhydrin (*see* Chapter 3, page 36) to reveal fingerprints.

cooperation, Lambourne examined hundreds of examples. He discovered that, during their production, parts of the standard pattern were altered when the latex slipped slightly on the mold, or when a piece of latex from a previous glove stuck to the mold. Even air bubbles could affect the pattern. Cloth gloves often have slight snags, tears, or holes, or detectable imperfections in the weave pattern. These come about through wear and tear or at the manufacturer's. Leather gloves can wrinkle or crease, or may have surface cracks and other signs of wear. It is possible to detect all these individual characteristics.

After lengthy tests and research, by 1971, Lambourne was confident that he knew enough to make a positive identification of a glove print. In January of that year, in London, a burglar alarm brought police to a crime scene, where

Defense attorney Barry Scheck interrogating forensic expert Dr. Henry Lee in the trial of O.J. Simpson for the murder of Nicole Brown Simpson and Ronald Goldman. The defense suggested that the parallel marks on the left leg of Goldman's bloodstained jeans were made by the boot of an unknown assailant.

Goldman's Boot

Goldman's Jeans

Forensic scientist revealing fingerprints on a scarf using a laser technique. The fingerprints are dusted with a dye, such as ninhydrin, which glows when exposed to laser light.

they arrested a man found climbing over a wall at the back of the building. Although he protested his innocence, investigators soon discovered a broken window. The fingerprint officer then found a glove print on a piece of glass.

Lambourne examined the print closely. He was positive that a damaged, left-hand, suede glove had left the print. Officers then examined the arrested man's gloves. They were made of sheepskin with a suede finish. The left glove's damaged surface matched exactly the print left on the glass. Though the burglar pleaded guilty, Lambourne was allowed to present his evidence in court. His testimony was accepted, and glove prints were established as evidence in English law.

In later cases, Lambourne successfully presented evidence involving gloves made from leather, PVC, rubber, and cotton twill. Police investigators all around the world have adopted his findings and even developed them further.

Fabric Prints

Fabrics other than gloves can also leave telltale evidence. In hit-and-run accidents, for example, the victim's clothes may leave impressions in dust on the vehicle's bodywork. In other situations, the criminal may have leaned a jacket sleeve on a dirty surface, or sat down somewhere. Clothed seat imprints can leave a detectable print on leather or PVC upholstery, and velvet can also retain an impression. At the very least, an examiner will be able to identify the type of fabric that left the impression at the crime scene. As with gloves, investigators can also detect peculiarities in the stitching, or signs of wear or damage, and trace them to a specific garment.

Ear Prints

Before breaking into a house, burglars and other intruders often listen closely at windows or doors to find out whether anyone is home. Without realizing it, they frequently leave a latent print of one ear on the surface. Although forensic investigators have been interested in ear prints for many years, it is only recently that anyone has done any research. There is now the possibility that a database can be built that will establish that no two ears—even those of otherwise identical twins—are identical. In the Netherlands, Cornelis van der Lugt has

CASE STUDY A GORILLA KILLER?

In *The Forensic Casebook* (2004), N.E. Genge describes a murder scene in Canada that puzzled and amazed investigators. Three people had been viciously stabbed to death in their bedrooms, and the lower rooms of the house had been ransacked. While dusting for fingerprints, the examining officer discovered prints 4 inches (10 centimeters) long. Equally strange, none of the prints showed any side detail, or any sign that the perpetrator had grasped objects between the fingers and thumb.

A junior officer suggested that it looked as if a trained gorilla had carried out the attacks. But there was no trace of animal hairs, and no characteristic odor. Had the killer worn gorilla gloves? Modeled latex, however, was unlikely to leave latent prints (*see* Chapter 3, page 33), unless they were smeared with sweat.

It seemed that the killer had deliberately staged the scene, constantly remembering to touch his hands to his face to make sure he left latent prints. The case was quickly solved when a local carnival costume company provided the credit card details of a man who had rented a gorilla costume on the day of the murders.

The imprint of Karl Stirk's ear on a door, part of the evidence that led to his conviction for the brutal murder of a female Irish law student in London in 1999.

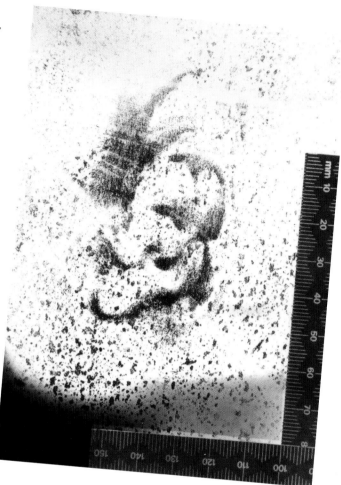

been studying the possibility, and recently a project has been set up in England, at the National Training Centre for Scientific Support to Crime Investigation. Already, some 2,000 ear prints have been collected.

However, initial progress has been followed by some setbacks in ear print research. In June 1996, David Kunze stood trial in Washington State, charged with murder, assault, and burglary. The main evidence against him was an ear print on a bedroom door, and he appealed against the admission of this evidence.

A Frye hearing (*see* Chapter 6, page 86) was held, at which Van de Lugt, among a number of other experts, testified, and the court concluded that the evidence was "generally accepted among the relevant scientific community." However, after several years in jail, Kunze was found not guilty on appeal.

In 1998, Mark Dallagher was sentenced to life imprisonment for the murder of Dorothy Wood, age 94, at her home in Huddersfield, England. British experts argued that he had left his ear print on a window of the house. A retrial was ordered by the Court of Appeal in 2003, after his defense lawyer offered new evidence. A report by Van der Lugt had stated that the print was "definitely not" Dallagher's, and a **DNA** analysis confirmed this. Dallagher went free in January 2004.

chapter 5

Impression Prints

Shoes and boots, as well as vehicle tires, can leave telltale impressions on surfaces, or in soft materials. These can be as important evidence as visible or latent fingerprints.

In almost every crime—with the obvious exception of hit-and-run cases—the criminal has to walk around while committing the crime. Inevitably, there will be numerous prints of the perpetrator's feet somewhere at the scene. One of the investigator's tasks is to find and record those prints.

Although the ridge patterns on the sole of the bare foot are said to be unique to each individual, in the same way as those on the fingers and palm, there has been little research carried out in this area. This is because fingerprinting—after it was originally established in India—has been developed mainly in Western nations, where criminals usually wear shoes.

Some maternity hospitals take prints from newborn babies' feet. This is to avoid any confusion. If they are transferred to a care unit with other babies, they can subsequently be identified. It is possible for the ridge patterns on the feet of two unrelated

◁ **To detect shoe and boot prints, it is often necessary to shine a light horizontally along the floor. The "Crime-Lite" is specially designed for this purpose, and has red, green, and blue filters for extra contrast on colored surfaces.**

63

babies to match. However, this happens among only a small proportion of the population.

In some cases, bloody bare foot marks have helped to identify the perpetrators of violent attacks. Like hands, bare feet also leave latent prints (*see* Chapter 3, page 33), which can be developed in the same way as fingerprints. Police forces, however, do not maintain database records of footprints. There have also been one or two cases in which a burglar, wearing gloves to avoid leaving fingerprints, has removed his shoes and socks, and left footprints for the police to find. Probably the most important use of footprints is identification of a murder victim when the killer has removed the hands in an attempt to conceal the person's identity. By searching the homes of missing persons, any smooth floors—particularly tiled bathroom floors—may reveal latent prints that match those on a dead body.

Shoes and Boots

Shoes and boots leave latent prints that can be very important evidence. They can be left in—or transferred from—newly painted surfaces, pools of blood, and other viscous (sticky, semi-fluid) liquids. It is also possible to get a detailed three-dimensional modeling of the sole from denser materials such as sand, mud, clay, wet cement, or even firm snow. A dusty floor can reveal visible tracks.

Burglars often kick in a door, leaving a clear dust print, particularly if they are wearing rubber-soled shoes. They may also use their legs to move a heavy object such as a safe, once again leaving footprints that can be photographed.

Indoors, it is possible to find latent prints from shoes. Investigators can develop these in the same way as fingerprints, but there are some difficulties. While fingerprints contain traces of sweat, shoe prints rarely do. The latent image is produced by the actual material of the sole, or by something that the criminal has walked in—most likely oil, or wax from a floor. In one Canadian case, police found a latent print on a TV screen. A neighbor had heard the criminal kick something that moved, so the investigator checked everything in the room until he found the print.

◁ **A forensic scientist uses a ruler to measure footprints made from a suspect's shoe. This can be compared with footprints found at a crime scene.**

CASE STUDY **A TELLING BRUISE**

During violent attacks, victims can be kicked and bruised. William Bodziak, the Federal Bureau of Investigation's top footwear expert, was called to the scene of the violent assault and murder of a young Florida girl. He found a bruise on her body, made by the heel of the killer's shoe. Bodziak recognized that a deck shoe had made the mark. The heel was worn down, and he could see where it had been stitched. "Stitching is done randomly," he said. "No two shoes are alike. Using the stitching holes, I was able to match the impression on that little girl's skin to the suspect's shoe."

An unusual pattern on a boot sole can quickly lead to identification of its maker, who may even be able to say where it was sold.

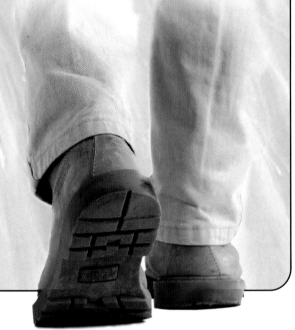

Examining the Scene of a Crime

Latent footwear prints can be found almost anywhere. In store robberies, the criminal is likely to leap onto and over the counter to get at the cash register. Victims struggling in cars may kick out and shatter the windshield, leaving prints on the fragments of glass, which can be reassembled. Prints in blood may be invisible to the eye on certain surfaces, but investigators must still search for them.

Most latent prints are not visible in direct light. They can be revealed, however, by shining an ordinary flashlight on the floor or other flat surface. Alternative light sources, such as **ultraviolet** or laser, can also be useful.

When investigators find prints, they dust them with normal fingerprint powder—black for light surfaces and gray for dark. They then photograph and lift the print. To lift the print, they lay strips of the standard 2-inch (5-centimeter) wide adhesive tape on to the dusted fingerprints. However, this is not always ideal: sheets of wider adhesive material are also used, although these can wrinkle. Rubberized sheets are favored, as they fit better to uneven surfaces, but—unlike transparent material—they preserve a reversed image.

Prints in dried blood are sprayed with **luminal** (a chemical that reveals invisible traces of blood), and then illuminated with ultraviolet light and photographed. In some cases, it is possible to remove an entire piece of the surface for detailed examination in the forensic laboratory.

An electrostatic mat can lift very faint prints found in dust on floors. A Japanese policeman, who moonlighted as a TV repairman, invented the technique in the 1960s. He noticed how the high-voltage source at the back of the television tube attracted dust. The mat consists of a sheet of metal foil sandwiched between two sheets of black **acetate** film. A weak, high-voltage current passed through the mat creates a static charge that attracts the dust. When illuminated at an angle and photographed, the black acetate can reveal enough detail to provide useful evidence. As only some of the dust is attracted at one time, more than one image can be lifted.

Taking Casts

Investigators first photograph impressed footprints and then take casts from them. These are known as **moulages** (*mool-aj*). The impressions are usually found outdoors, and can degrade quite rapidly, particularly in heavy rain. If the material is loose, the investigator often sprays a cloud of transparent acrylic paint over—but not into—the impression to stabilize it. Sometimes, investigators even use common hairspray. Firm impressions in mud or clay can be cast as they are, but in many cases they have to place a frame around the print before pouring in the casting material.

Prints in snow can be stabilized by first spraying them with a red-colored product called Snow Print Wax. The wax also acts as an insulator, preventing the heat generated by the casting material from melting any details in the impression. The red coloration also makes the cast easier to photograph.

Investigators have also used a light dusting of talcum powder before taking a cast in snow.

Originally, police used **plaster of paris** to take casts, but now they generally use "dental stone," which is almost identical to plaster of paris chemically, but is harder and sets more quickly. Like plaster, it is mixed with water to a consistency similar to thin batter. Then it is gently poured over the back of—for example—the mixing spoon into the impression. The best method is to use a bag like the kind used to pipe cake icing, slowly squeezing the mixture out.

There can be complications when taking casts in snow—because it will probably start to melt. Snow Print Wax must be kept relatively warm, at room temperature, for successful spraying; otherwise the nozzle will clog. Dental stone cannot be mixed with warm water—it must be mixed with the coldest water possible, which makes it much more difficult to mix and squeeze out. Plaster and dental stone both generate heat as they set, which can destroy fine detail. Another method involves sulfur powder. The powder is melted with hot water to produce a rubber-like material that hardens immediately on contact with the cold snow, capturing all the details.

Recently, investigators have very successfully used a material known as **silastomer** (*sil-as-toh-mah*) to take casts from sloping surfaces, where other materials would run to one end of the casting frame. It is mixed with hardener immediately before use, and sets within seconds. Unlike other similar materials, silastomer is not adhesive, so it is possible to lift it from the impression without damaging it.

As a cast begins to harden, investigators mark the date, time, location, and other key information into its upper surface. Depending on the material used and the local conditions, hardening can take from twenty minutes to an hour. The cast is then lifted, and any dirt or grass sticking to it is later removed in the forensic laboratory. The cast is completely hard in about twenty-four hours.

Following a Trail

While police must match a single print to a suspect's footwear, a trail of prints can provide valuable information about the perpetrator and his behavior. The distance between prints indicates the individual's height, while the depth of

A cast of a boot print, probably made with liquid sulfur, taken from a crime scene. The scale measures the size of the boot.

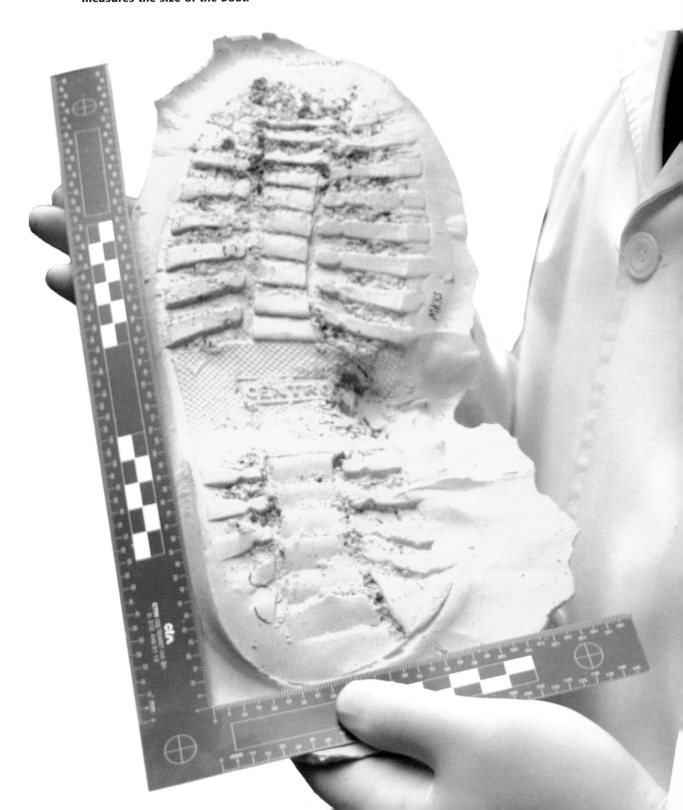

impression in a soft material gives an approximate measure of weight.

The nature of the prints is also revealing. Was the individual moving calmly, placing the whole foot down, or creeping on tiptoe? Some of the prints may be clearer on one side than the other, indicating that the person was leaning sideways at that point. Usually, when an individual is running, only the toe of the shoe leaves an impression, and, in soft ground, throws up a ridge or spray of material behind it.

Even a poor trail of prints—which cannot be used as evidence—can show what direction the perpetrator went when fleeing the scene. This trail may lead to a better set of prints—at the scene of a second crime, or even where the getaway car was parked. Tire impressions from the car can be identified and used in evidence.

Nowadays, many criminals wear athletic training shoes. Each model that goes on sale has a characteristic patterned sole. Forensic laboratories maintain extensive databases of these patterns, which help them to identify a specific model very quickly. Manufacturers willingly provide information when a pattern is not yet on a database. In particular, they can also tell investigators how many shoes of that type they manufactured, where they were distributed, and even how many of each size.

Boot Prints that Led Nowhere

The "Zodiac killer," a serial murderer who terrorized the Bay Area in California in 1968–1970, has never been caught. Napa Valley police, however, identified the shoes he wore, and made a close guess at his size and weight.

On September 27, 1969, the Zodiac stabbed Cecelia Shephard to death at a picnic spot by Lake Berryessa, and severely wounded her companion, Bryan Hartnell. When police arrived at the scene, they found a trail of deep footprints in the sand, leading to the site of the crime and back up to the road.

The investigating officer ordered his heaviest deputy to walk beside the track: he weighed about 210 pounds (95 kilograms), but his prints were not as deep as

◁ **Criminals seldom leave prints of their naked feet at the crime scene. In this unusual case of homicide in Southeast Asia, the assailant was obviously barefoot, and has left clear footprints for the police investigators to pursue.**

those left by the killer. The officer calculated that the Zodiac killer must weigh at least 220 pounds (99.8 kilograms). The clear heel prints indicated that he had not run but walked away calmly.

Police took casts and identified the manufacturer from an unusual circle in the sole prints. The prints were made by an ankle-boot called "Wing Walker." Unfortunately, the manufacturers had produced more than a million pairs as part of a government contract, and 103,700 pairs had been distributed to United States Air Force and Navy installations on the West Coast. The police wondered whether the killer was connected to the military—but the case remains unsolved.

Prints in the Sand

Native trackers possess an uncanny ability to follow a trail. In his book *Mostly Murder* (1959), the distinguished Scottish pathologist Sir Sydney Smith (1883–1969) described a typical case. In the 1920s, he was working as an adviser to the Egyptian government, when the body of a local postman was found in the desert outside Cairo. He had been shot in the head.

The commandant of the city police enlisted the aid of Bedouin trackers. (The Bedouin are nomadic tribes of the Arabian, Syrian, or North African deserts.) "They could without difficulty spot the tracks of different persons they knew," wrote Smith, "and could tell whether a person … was running or walking, whether loaded or free, and so on."

Although the police could see nothing, the Bedouin detected the footprints of a man, who had been wearing sandals, leading to the point where the body was found. They traced them back approximately 40 yards (36.5 meters), where they found marks left by someone kneeling. Nearby, they picked up an empty .303 rifle cartridge. After killing the postman, the Bedouin said, the man had taken off his sandals and ran barefoot to a road. There, they found traces of a car and the prints of four people wearing boots. The car tracks led them to a fort, where six members of the Camel Corps were camped.

Next morning, all six soldiers were marched barefoot, several times, over an

▷ **Police taking a cast of a tire track near the scene of a reported sniper shooting in Hammond, Indiana, in 2006.**

POLICE
EVIDENCE
DO NOT REMOVE

CASE STUDY | TELLTALE SNEAKER PRINT

When Richard Ramirez, the Night Stalker (*see* Chapter 3, page 45), began to terrorize the Los Angeles suburbs in 1984, the police did not at first connect his crimes. In Montebello, on February 25, 1985, a young girl was abducted and assaulted. While conducting an investigation of the crime, the police found a distinctive shoe print in wet cement.

On March 28, 1985, the bodies of Vincent Zazzara and his wife were discovered at their home in Whittier. The perpetrator had forced a window to gain entry and left several large shoe prints in the flowerbed. Experts identified the shoe as an Avia model 440, size 11½.

Whittier was in a different county than Montebello, so it was not until police from different jurisdictions realized that they were investigating the same killer that they made the connection. They discovered that only 1,354 pairs of this model of shoe had been made, and only six pairs had been sold on the West Coast. Of these six, only one pair had been size 11½.

On August 31, 1985, police arrested Ramirez after a chase and found he was wearing a pair of Avias, model 440, size 11½.

Clearly defined prints of a boot, and a dog's paw, in sand. Before a cast can be taken, the soft material must be fixed with a light spray of transparent acrylic paint—or even common hair spray.

area of smooth sand. Each time, the trackers identified the same man.

Unfortunately, the authorities did not think this evidence was strong enough for a conviction. Smith, however, showed that the fatal bullet had been fired from this man's gun. It turned out that the postman had been having an affair with the soldier's sister. The soldier killed him to avenge his family's honor.

Inside the Shoe

The interior of footwear rarely provides latent prints of the bare sole, but it can provide other valuable leads. The foot generates heat and sweat, and, after someone has worn shoes or boots for some time, they become molded to the shape of the person's feet.

It is possible to take casts from inside the footwear. Sir Sydney Smith pioneered the technique using a mixture of gelatin and glycerin to create a cast. In 1937, two very similar break-ins occurred in Falkirk, Scotland. In each case, a pair of shoes was left, neatly placed beside the drainpipe that the criminal had climbed to get in to the premises. After a third break-in, the intruder was caught in his socks. Police found a pair of boots beside the drainpipe. The man admitted they were his, but denied he had committed the two previous crimes.

Smith found that all three pairs revealed the same signs of wear. The right upper bulged over the big toe, and the sole was very worn, while the left sole was not. He made casts and announced—without seeing the suspect—that the owner of the shoes had a deformed left leg and foot, probably the result of having polio when young. (Polio is an acute infectious disease that causes the skeletal muscles to shrivel.) He walked with a characteristic limp, with an outward swing of the left toe, which dragged along the ground. It was very likely, Smith concluded, that the man also suffered a curvature of the spine, because his pelvis dipped to the left. Smith was correct on all these points, and the perpetrator was convicted of all three robberies.

Barefoot Morphology

Since 1948, the Royal Canadian Mounted Police has been developing a related technique called barefoot morphology. With use over time, parts of the insoles of footwear become compressed and stained, particularly by the toepads, the ball of the foot, and the heel. It is also possible to detect blisters, calluses, and scars. Inked impressions of the bare feet of any suspect can then be compared with the impressions on the insole. Investigators also photograph the insole and soles of the suspect's feet, as well as the top and sides. These can be compared with very worn areas on the shoe's upper side.

The bloody footprints at the scene of the murder of Nicole Brown Simpson and Ronald Goldman. They were identified as having been made by a Bruno Magli shoe. O. J. Simpson denied owning such a pair, but photographs later showed him wearing a pair.

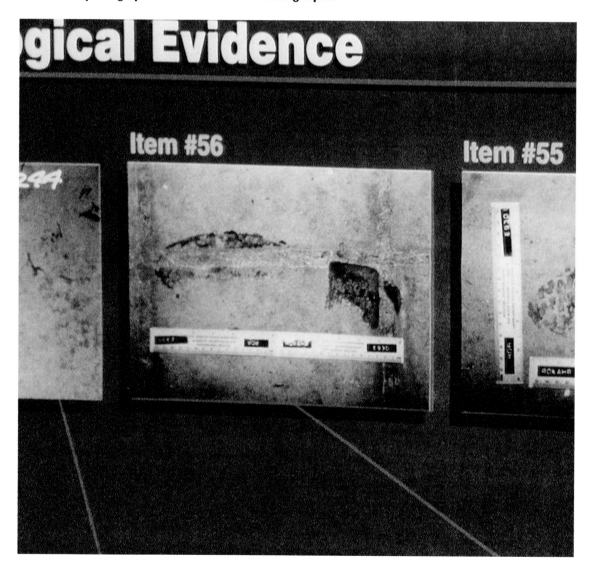

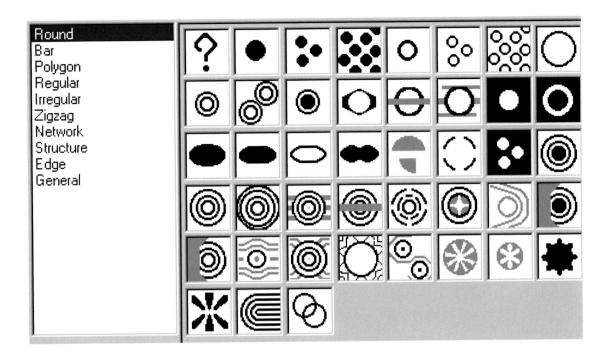

Shoe prints and tire marks are coded by identifying elemental pattern features. This computer screen graphic shows many types of round-shaped shoe tread patterns. Identifying the type of tread and manufacture of shoe can help identify the wearer.

In recent years, military officials have started taking barefoot prints of military flight personnel. If their bodies are unrecognizable after an aircraft crash, their footwear may have survived, and be enough to identify them.

Tire Tracks

Many criminals use cars or vans to get to the scene of a crime. Criminals often travel many miles in search of a suitable victim. Inevitably, the vehicle has to be parked somewhere, either while the criminals carry out the crime, or to dump possible evidence in a remote spot.

Whether stationary or moving, all vehicles leave valuable trace evidence. There may be a patch of oil at the site, cigarette butts, leftover traces of food, or discarded tissues that can be analyzed for DNA. In a quick getaway, a vehicle can leave marks when it strikes a tree or wall. Equally important are the car's tire tracks. These tracks may leave impressions in dirt, clay, mud or sand, snow, or other materials at the crime site—even cow or horse droppings. They may be prints transferred from a pool of blood, oil, or spilt paint, or from a patch of thin mud. In hit-and-run incidents or traffic accidents, the tires can leave clear bruise impressions on the victim's body.

The tracks left by moving four-wheeled cars, vans, and trucks—or bicycles and motorbikes—are usually clear only when a vehicle has turned a corner, or is not traveling straight. Normally, when a vehicle moves in a straight line, the rear tire tracks are superimposed on those in front, producing an inaccurate impression that cannot be presented as evidence in court.

Sample Analysis

Investigators photograph transferred prints in blood, paint, mud, or similar materials, or those on the victim's body. It is rarely possible for them to lift the surface with the prints and take it back to the forensic laboratory. Although photographs are only two-dimensional, it is still possible to compare them with similar prints from a suspect's car, or with sample tires.

If the mud is the right consistency, impressions may be deep enough for investigators to measure the depth of the tire's tread on the spot. The next step, whatever the material, is to take a cast—in the same way that footprint casts are taken. If the impression is in dry dirt or sand, it may be necessary to take a preliminary cast with a solution of **shellac** (*shel-lack*), or a similar plastic material. From this cast, investigators then make a plaster cast. There is one disadvantage to this technique. The first shellac cast is a copy of the tire pattern, but this is not suitable for presentation in evidence, as it is too fragile. The second, plaster cast is a copy of the imprint—so it will be reversed left-to-right, and high-to-low, which makes it harder for the jury to compare it with evidential photographs.

In the Laboratory

At the forensic laboratory—or even on site—an examiner can obtain a lot of information about the tire, from either an impression or a flat print. First of all,

An investigator analyzes the precise variation in a tire pattern taken from a cast. Close laboratory examination will allow him to examine wear and tear on the tread, the width of the tire, and its age.

tires are made in different widths for different makes of vehicle. They quickly show signs of wear, and may also have been damaged in some way.

When a cast is available, investigators can determine the age of the tire from the depth of the tread. If they can identify the make of the vehicle, an unusual width of print can indicate whether it was loaded—perhaps estimating the number of people in the vehicle or load weight. It may even be possible to tell where, exactly, the load was placed in the vehicle. Unevenness in the suspension results in changes in the pattern of wear from one side of the tire to the other. Scrub, which happens to tires when the front wheels are not properly aligned, can also be important evidence.

Tires usually carry the manufacturer's name and logo, as well as the tire's dimensions. These details are usually on the wall of the tire, so they are unlikely to leave an impression. The unmistakable element, however, is the tire's tread. Every manufacturer has its own distinctive tread patterns. Each claims its treads have the best grip and water-shedding characteristics. A variety of tread patterns are available for use with different vehicles, such as cars, trucks, motorbikes, and bicycles. Forensic laboratories maintain a comprehensive database of tire tracks and, as with shoes, the manufacturers or dealers willingly provide further information about which tires are normally fitted on which vehicles, when and where they were sold, and so on.

Completing the Puzzle

With all this information, the investigator can identify a suspect's vehicle. However, this proves only that the suspect usually drives the vehicle. It does not prove that he was present at the scene of the crime. The suspect may claim that, on the date of the crime, he had loaned his car to a friend, or even that it was stolen and later recovered. Nevertheless, tire tracks are another important piece of evidence in the investigation jigsaw. Apart from extensive records of tire tracks held by many official forensic laboratories, there are now a number of independent organizations in the United States providing identification services. And William Bodziack, the FBI investigator, now retired, teaches a five-day course on impression evidence, including footwear and tires.

The Case of Vijay Cooppen

In the early hours of March 31, 1990, British police found the body of Jini Cooppen in a yard in Brixton, south London. She had been strangled, but there were no signs of a struggle at the scene. It seemed probable that she had been killed elsewhere and brought to the site. Interest centered on tire marks close by the body.

A typical Goodyear Vogue tire. The various patterns of tread are specific to every manufacturer, and provide valuable evidence in identification.

BOBBY JOE LONG

Between 1980 and 1983, an unknown man terrorized communities along the Miami coast of Florida, attacking, robbing, and murdering people in their homes. From tracks at two of the crime scenes, the police discovered that the serial killer was driving a sedan with two unusual rear tires. One was a Goodyear Vogue, an expensive type of tire used only on Cadillacs. The other was fitted the wrong way, with the white wall facing inward.

In November, the killer assaulted a girl, but then spared her life. She gave the police a detailed description of her attacker. On November 17, 1984, police arrested Bobby Joe Long, age thirty-one, and charged him with nine counts of first-degree murder, together with felony counts of abduction and rape. Examination of the tires on his car established that it had been used in at least two of the murders.

The immediate suspect was Jini's husband, Vijay Cooppen. The forensic examiner's report stated that the vehicle which made the impressions had a Dunlop tire on the left front wheel, and a Goodyear tire on the right. Coopen's Volvo car had three Dunlop tires and one Goodyear tire. When police made inquiries near his home, they confirmed that the tires had been fitted to Cooppen's car on the morning of March 30. When police compared the two front tires with the impressions at the crime scene, they found a perfect match. However, this evidence in itself was

A French forensic scientist comparing a cast of a tire from a crime scene with a sample from the manufacturer. Precise details in measurement are vital before positive identification.

CASE STUDY   A PIONEERING CASE

In his memoirs, the famous (and infamous) French detective François Vidocq (1775–1857) records the first instance of a cast being taken. At the scene of an attempted murder, he found several very clear boot prints. By taking a plaster cast, he matched the impression with the boots of an arrested suspect. This evidence, together with other traces discovered at the scene, secured him a conviction.

not enough for a conviction, so the police traced the batch of Goodyear tires that included the one fitted to Cooppen's Volvo.

It turned out that the manufacturers used only twelve molds to make this particular type and size of tire. Of these twelve, only two produced the relevant tread pattern. Goodyear had exported most of them to Holland, though a small quantity had gone to dealers in Britain.

It was extremely unlikely that another car, fitted with a Dunlop tire on the left front and an unusual type of Goodyear on the right, could have been in south London on the night of March 30. Police completed their investigation when Vijay's five-year-old son told them that his father had been out of the house for five hours on the night in question.

Unknown Arsonists

During the first week of February, 2006, fires were started by unknown arsonists at five Baptist churches in Bibb County, Alabama. The only clue discovered by investigators was a set of tire tracks found at one of the sites. After extensive inquiries, and the inspection of some 500 vehicles, the type of tire was traced to a local store. A set of these tires had been purchased by a Mrs. Cloyd for her sports utility vehicle, and suspicion fell on her twenty-year-old son Matthew. He subsequently confessed, and he and two fellow college students told investigators that they had started the fires as a joke.

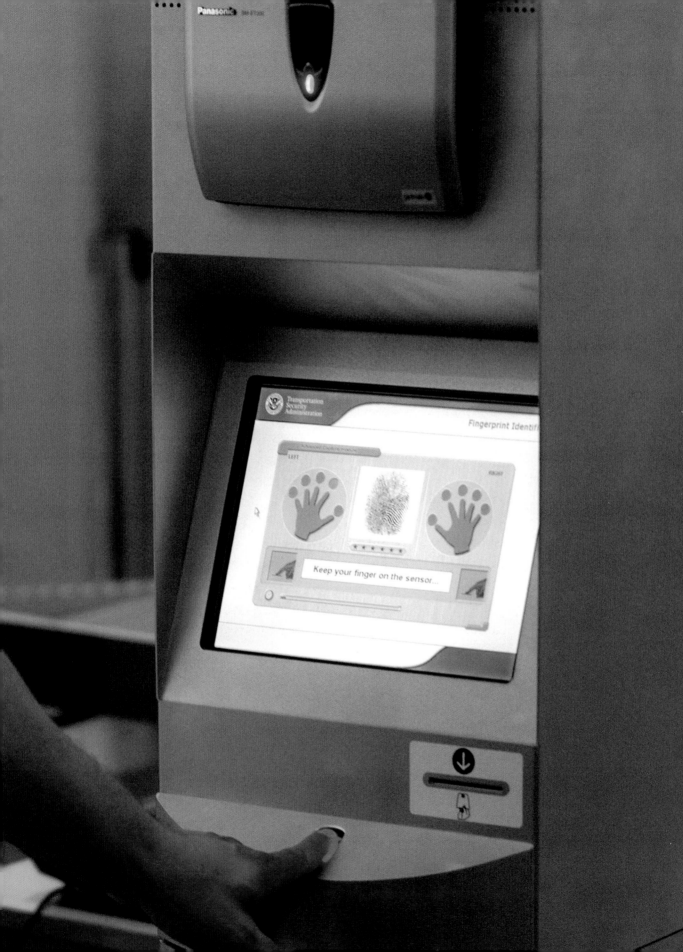

chapter 6

A Question of Evidence

Expert scientific opinion is essential when testimony is given in court. Specific rules have been established in law, but the defense can still challenge the validity of evidence.

For a century, courts of law have accepted fingerprints as evidence of positive identification. This confidence is based on the theory that no two individuals, anywhere in the world, have identical prints. Yet, this remains just that— a theory that cannot be proved conclusively by experiment.

On its own, a fingerprint is not enough evidence to convict a person. A suspect's prints may match those found at a crime scene, but this proves only that the person was present at the scene at one time or another. Unless the suspect, when faced with this apparently incriminating evidence, confesses to the crime, the authorities need other physical or circumstantial evidence to establish a case for prosecution.

Nevertheless, the testimony of a fingerprint expert can have a strong influence on a jury in court. In the early days of fingerprint evidence (*see* Chapter 2), prosecuting lawyers and

◁ **A close-up of a screen and iris reader used by the Transportation Security Administration at Minneapolis-St. Paul International Airport. The kiosk provides biometric information to identify travelers.**

expert witnesses had to explain every detail of fingerprinting technique, so that the judge and jury could understand the evidence. Before long, most people understood that each person had unique fingerprints, so this detailed explanation was no longer needed. The expert's testimony and the records presented to the court were enough. Recently, however, defense lawyers—particularly in the United States—have begun to question the legal validity of fingerprint evidence.

The Frye and Daubert Standards

In the United States, two cases heard in higher courts established precedents in U.S. law. The first case was *Frye v. United States*, 1923. The defense wanted to prevent **polygraph** (*pol-ee-graf*), or "lie detector," evidence being presented in court. The District of Columbia Trial Court approved this motion, and the D.C. Appellate Court affirmed it.

The polygraph had been introduced only two years previously, and the view of the courts was that, as a new type of scientific evidence, the polygraph had not yet "gained general acceptance." In fact, polygraph evidence is still inadmissible today. J. Edgar Hoover, former director of the Federal Bureau of Investigation (FBI), famously ordered his agents to "throw that box into Biscayne Bay."

Most state courts adopted the Frye Standard and added further requirements. For example, the state of Hawaii added five additional requirements, including that "the evidence will add to the common understanding of the jury," the "underlying theory is generally accepted as valid," and "procedures used are generally accepted as reliable." In 1975, however, the U.S. Supreme Court drew up a set of Federal Rules of Evidence, which Congress made law. Individual states used these rules as guidance when drawing up their own rules about what could and could not be admitted as evidence in court.

Then, in 1993, came the case of *Daubert v. Merrell Dow Pharmaceuticals*. The parents of children born with physical defects brought the case on the grounds that the drug Bendection, produced by Dow, was to blame for their children's disabilities. The U.S. Supreme Court rejected the Frye Standard of "general acceptance" in jurisdictions governed by the Federal Rules, and offered new guidelines—the Daubert Standard—relating to new types of scientific evidence (*see opposite page*).

After the Supreme Court's ruling, some people feared that all sorts of scientific opinion would now be admissible in court. However, to this day, courts have strictly applied the Daubert Standard, firmly rejecting what is called **junk science**, or quasi-scientific opinion.

Unscientific Evidence

But what does all this have to do with fingerprint evidence? Since the first years of the twentieth century, fingerprinting has certainly gained general acceptance. It is definitely not a new technique. However, is it truly scientific? As already stated, the uniqueness of an individual's prints is a matter of theory, and in scientific practice it is necessary to carry out experiments specifically designed

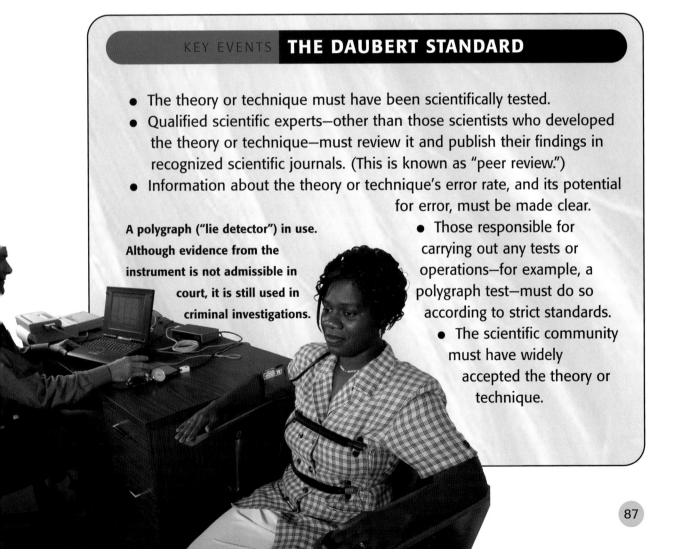

KEY EVENTS **THE DAUBERT STANDARD**

- The theory or technique must have been scientifically tested.
- Qualified scientific experts—other than those scientists who developed the theory or technique—must review it and publish their findings in recognized scientific journals. (This is known as "peer review.")
- Information about the theory or technique's error rate, and its potential for error, must be made clear.
- Those responsible for carrying out any tests or operations—for example, a polygraph test—must do so according to strict standards.
- The scientific community must have widely accepted the theory or technique.

A polygraph ("lie detector") in use. Although evidence from the instrument is not admissible in court, it is still used in criminal investigations.

to disprove a theory. Only when every conceivable experiment fails can the theory be accepted. As far as the Daubert Standard is concerned, the technique of fingerprinting has been tested over a long period, peer reviewed, and widely accepted. However, its known or potential error rate cannot be determined. In a number of recent cases, clever defense lawyers, using the Daubert Standard, have asked the court to rule fingerprint evidence inadmissible on the grounds that it was not scientific.

By 2006, more than forty such "Daubert motions" relating to fingerprint evidence have been denied by the court, withdrawn by the defense, or declared inadmissible by a higher court.

Points of Comparison

The fingerprints of many individuals could be superficially similar, differing only in minor details. The expert's job in court is to show that a sufficient number of details in the accused person's prints and those taken from the scene of the crime are identical.

The French forensic scientist Dr. Edmond Locard was the first person to suggest that twelve compatibility points were enough to match the identity of a print. Today, however, different countries have their own standards. English law requires a minimum of sixteen characteristics in the ridge patterns of a single finger or palm print, or ten on each digit in the case of two prints. The probability of two persons having the same ridge pattern is one in 10,000,000,000,000—more than 1,000 times the population of the world.

Modern French law requires seventeen matching points, while Greece, Switzerland, and Spain require twelve. Sweden accepts ten. The United States abandoned any formal standard requirement in 1973, but the FBI generally accepts ten compatibility points.

The identification of fingerprints by the computerized Automated Fingerprint Identification System (AFIS), or similar systems, results in evidence that would be difficult to explain simply in court. The computer plots the relative position of specific ridge patterns, such as points where the ridges divide, and the direction of the ridge at these points. The computer produces a diagram, or map, of the various identifiable features that is very different from the normal analysis of a fingerprint. It then compares this map with the records on the database, and

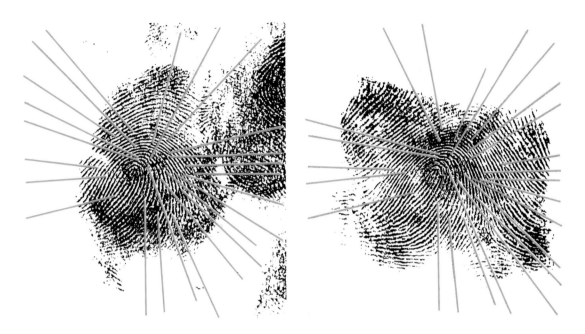

A computer "map" analysis of a fingerprint and its partial impression. Twenty-four positive points of comparison have been identified by the computer.

presents a ranked list of about twenty of the most likely matches. Examiners can then compare the print from the crime scene with those on this shortlist in the usual way. If they discover a positive match, they present it as evidence in court.

Mistaken Identity

Some recent cases have highlighted the need for extreme care when using the fingerprinting technique. An examiner, anxious to obtain a positive result, may decide that one print looks so similar to another that it must be identical. This is known as **cognitive bias**. In 1997, Stephan Cowans was accused of shooting a police officer while fleeing a robbery in Roxbury, Massachusets, and was sentenced to thirty-five years in jail. Two witnesses, including the wounded officer, testified that Cowans was the assailant. A fingerprint on a glass mug provided further evidence. Experts testified positively that it was Cowans' print. For six years, Cowans worked in prison to raise enough money to have the evidence tested for DNA. Analysis of the latent print showed that it was not his, and he was eventually released.

The terrorist bomb that exploded in the rush-hour in Madrid, Spain, in March 2004, killed 192 people and maimed many more.

Also in 1997, a woman was murdered in a house in Kilmarnock, Scotland. Police officer Shirley McKie was accused of having left her thumbprint inside the house—breaking a rule of crime scene procedure. McKie denied having entered the house, but in the following year she was arrested and charged with perjury. At her trial in May 1999, two experts testified in her defense, and she was found not guilty. The Scottish Criminal Record Office would not admit the error, but in February 2006, McKie was awarded £750,000 ($1,320,000 U.S.) in compensation.

In March 2004, terrorists exploded bombs on trains in Madrid, Spain, killing many people. Investigators found a fingerprint and sent it to the FBI, which reported that AFIS had detected a 100 percent positive match. The print on file belonged to Brandon Mayfield, an Oregon lawyer. However, experts in the Spanish police disagreed, and they eventually tracked down another man. In January 2006, the U.S. Department of Justice faulted the FBI Latent Print Unit for careless work, but exonerated them of more serious allegations. It concluded that the misidentification in this case was not an indication that fingerprint evidence generally was unreliable. The FBI claims to have made only one error

▷ **Many security access systems have now introduced scanners for the positive identification of authorized persons.**

in identification every eleven years. Brandon Mayfield's case was the first time in eighty-four years that the FBI had reported a positive result before discovering the error.

Fingerprinting—and its related applications—remains the most useful of all methods for the positive identification of an individual. It is still considered the most important technique in forensic investigation, even more than DNA typing, and has resulted in more cases being solved than all other methods combined. The science of fingerprinting is so well-established, there is now an international call for fingerprints to be included on identity cards.

PROCEDURE **PRIZED PRINTS**

Today, no rigorous experimental program has been carried out to prove, or disprove, the theory of fingerprint evidence. There have been, however, a few random, uncontrolled experiments. For example, in 1939, the British weekly newspaper *News of the World* ran a competition to test the infallibility of fingerprinting. The paper reproduced five enlarged prints of the fingertips of a male hand and five of a female hand. The newspaper offered a prize of £1,000 ($4,000 U.S.) to any man who could produce an identical set of prints, and the same amount to any woman. Nobody claimed the prize, but this "experiment" covered only a relatively small population sample.

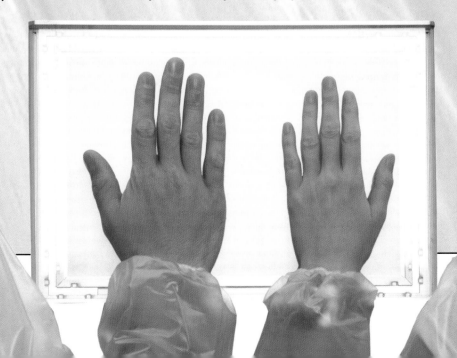

Glossary

acetate a transparent film

alibi the defense by an accused person of having been elsewhere at the time an alleged offense was committed

amino acids nitrogen-containing compounds that join together to build into proteins; there are about 20 common amino acids, ten of which are essential to the human diet (see "proteins")

anthropometric referring to the science used to measure the physical differences between people, such as the size and shape of the head, facial features, body shape, etc.

archaeologist someone who studies the remains of ancient human life and activities

classification the method by which things are grouped and separated based on common or different characteristics

cognitive bias "cognitive" means "knowing"—and when analysts know what they are looking for, they may be so anxious to detect it—"biased"—that they identify something else by mistake

cyanoacrylate (*sie-uh-noh-ak-ruh-leyt*) the true name for superglue

dactylography the original name for the analysis and study of fingerprints

DNA deoxyribonucleic (dee-oxy-ry-bo-nu-kle-ik) acid; the substance found in the cells of living things that contain the genes, which control heredity

digits the fingers and thumbs

ferrous material containing iron

iodine vapor a purple-brown poisonous vapor produced by heating crystals of the element iodine

junk science "scientific" opinion that is offered by self-professed "experts"— generally by the defense—and which is not supported by rigorous experimental evidence

latent prints prints that are present as trace evidence, but not visible to the naked eye

luminal a chemical compound that glows in ultraviolet light and is closely related to veronal (barbitone)

microscopist someone who uses a microscope

moulages (*mool-aj*) a mold, as of a footprint, made for use in a criminal investigation

ninhydrin (*nin-hahy-drin*) also known as Triketohydrindene-hydrate; a chemical that is used to detect amino acids

nonferrous material not containing any iron

papillary ridges small ridges on the surface of the skin

patent prints prints that are visible to the naked eye

plaster of paris a white insoluble powder that is used to take casts

polygraph lie detector—an instrument that measures pulse rate, blood pressure, rhythm of the chest in breathing, and electrical disturbances created by the activity of the sweat glands in the hands. The machine draws graphs that record states of stress. The person being interrogated is asked a succession of questions. To some of these —such as name, address, and other known facts— he or she will answer truthfully. However, a lie may be accompanied by a change in breathing or heartbeat, and increased sweating. The polygraph is unreliable, as the person may already be under stress from other causes, may believe his or her own lies, or be an experienced criminal

proteins very large group of compounds that are essential to life and an essential part of the animal diet. Proteins are necessary components of many parts of all animal and plant bodies. DNA provides the code for their manufacture in the cell. The principal sources are meat, cheese, eggs, cereals, nuts, and beans

radii measuring from the center of a sphere to its outer boundary

radioactive giving out alpha particles, electrons, and gamma-radiation (very short wavelength x-rays)

shellac a varnish prepared from a resin (lac), which is produced when insects puncture the bark of certain varieties of tree

silastomer silicone rubber. There are many different types of silicone. A silicone is a synthetic compound similar to a natural substance, but with many of the carbon atoms replaced by silicon atoms

silver nitrate colorless chemical, $AgNO_3$, made by dissolving silver in nitric acid, and producing crystals from the solution. It is very soluble in water, and reacts with the salt and amino acids in sweat, releasing very tiny particles of metallic silver as a black residue, particularly when exposed to light

sweat pores small holes in the human skin that release sweat to cool the body to stop it overheating

typhoid serious fever produced by infection with Salmonella typhosa, a bacterium that generally enters the body from contaminated water

ultraviolet a radioactive wavelength just beyond the visible spectrum

Learn More About

A wealth of information on fingerprinting, as well as a broader look at forensic science, is available from the various media. Listed below are books and Web sites that link to government bureaus, professional bodies, reports, magazine and newspaper articles, and other sources.

Books

Beaven, Colin, *Fingerprints*. London: Fourth Estate, 2002.

Cherrill, Frederick, *Fingerprints Never Lie*. New York: Macmillan, 1954.

Fisher, Barry A.J., *Techniques of Crime Scene Investigation*. New York: Elsevier, 1992.

Fletcher, Tony, *Memories of Murder*. London: Grafton, 1987.

Forrest, D.W., *Francis Galton: The Life and Work of a Victorian Genius*. New York: Tiplinger, 1974.

Genge, N.E., *The Forensic Casebook*. New York: Ballantine, 2004.

Henry, Sir Edward, *Classification and Uses of Fingerprints*. London: HMSO, 1937, 8th edition.

Lambourne, Gerald, *The Fingerprint Story*. London: Harrap, 1984.

Lee, Henry C., and Gaesslen, R.E. (eds), *Advances in Fingerprint Technology*. New York: Elsevier, 1991.

Lyle, D.P., *Forensics for Dummies*. Hoboken, NJ: Wiley Publishing, 2004.

Ragle, Larry, *Crime Scene*. New York: Avon Books. 2002.

Sengoopta, Chandak, *Imprint of the Raj*. London: Macmillan, 2003.

Theoharis, Athan G. (ed), *The FBI*. New York: Checkmark Books, 2000.

U.S. Department of Justice, Federal Bureau of Investigation. *The Science of Fingerprints*. Washington, D.C. no date.

Web Sites

Creative Chemistry: Fingerprinting— www.creative-chemistry.org.uk/activities/ fingerprinting.htm

Federal Bureau of Investigation—Fingerprints: www.fbi.gov/hq/cjisd/cjis.htm

Fingerprinting: www.cyberbee.com/whodunnit/fp.html

Fingerprinting and Palmar Dermatoglyphics: www.edcampbell.com/PalmD-History.htm

Integrated Automated Fingerprint Identification System (IAFIS): www.fbi.gov/hq/cjisd/iafis.htm

Onin—Forensic Sciences, Fingerprints: www.onin.com

Reach out Michigan (Schools exercise)— Fingerprinting: www.reachoutmichigan.org/ funexperiments/agesubject/lessons/prints. html

Ridges and Furrows: www.ridgesandfurrows.homestead.com/

Who Dunnit?: www.cyberbee.com/whodunnit/crime.html

About the Author

Brian Innes began his professional career as a research biochemist in industry. He later transferred to chemical journalism, and was subsequently creative director and deputy chairman of Orbis Publishing, a leading London publisher. His first book on a criminal subject, *The Book of Outlaws*, was published in 1966.

Since 1990 he has concentrated on forensic science, beginning with a succession of articles for the weekly magazine *Real Life Crimes*. His more recent books include *Bodies of Evidence, Profile of a Criminal Mind, Body in Question,* and *Serial Killers*. He is a member of the Crime Writers' Association, and chairman of the panel of judges for their Gold Dagger award for non-fiction writing. He currently lives in the south of France.

Quoted Sources

p. 16—Anon, *Memoriales de una Vita en la Policia* (mar del Plata, 1905), from "Fifty Years of Dactyloscopy in Argentina," by Antonio Herrero, *Finger Print Magazine*, 1943

p. 66—*Hard Evidence* (New York, Dell, 1995), by David Fisher.

p. 72—*Mostly Murder* (New York: Dorset Press, 1989), by Sir Sydney Smith

p. 86 (1)—*The FBI* (New York, 2000), ed. Athan G. Theodaris et al

p. 86 (2)—Hawaii Statute §706-603: Mental and medical examination; deoxyribonucleic acid collection

Index